THE EURO IS TO BLAME
Economics for Spanish people

ii

THE EURO IS TO BLAME
Economics for Spanish people

Luke Fog

Luke Fog
2015

iv

Original Title: La Culpa es del Euro. Economía para españoles.

Translated from original Spanish by Simon Hill

First Edition: July de 2015

Copyright © 2015 by Luke Fog

First printing: 2015

ISBN 978-1-326-47683-0

Luke Fog

For those who dream of a better world

Contents

Acknowledgments

I would like to give special thanks to my wife and my children for the support and the affection they give me every day. I have been very lucky. Thank you. Also to my parents and my brothers and sisters for everything they have given me, especially the education and the training I have received.

Finally, I would like to thank my teachers, my colleagues and friends for what they have taught me.

To all of them, for the time we have spent together.

Preface

The purpose of this book is to make a modest contribution to popular knowledge of economic science. I don't want to be too technical when talking about the crisis and I try to be as educational as possible, so that everyone can understand it. Unlike other books on the subject written by economics teachers and professors, it is my intention to add knowledge of the market, especially of the real estate sector which, because of its cyclical nature and because it is in the eye of the hurricane in this crisis, provides important information.

Neither do I intend to be dogmatic. There are ideas about which I have changed my mind over the last few years. Here I reflect what I believe to be most correct from the point of view of normative economics and what I know about positive economics. By the first I understand that which is the subject of political debate and on which empirical experience is more debatable; the second is understood to be something which is more or less Science, because empirical experience demonstrates that the results of actions undertaken are usually the same.

The contents of the first part of the book have a certain similarity with the way in which John Kenneth Galbraith explained the Crash of 1929 or his "A short history of financial euphoria"[1]. It is, however, not as descriptive, nor does it focus so much on the facts as on the explanation of the economic theory linked to those facts.

My studies on company management and Economics at the Chicago Booth Business School at the University of Chicago, together with the economic crisis and my direct contact with the real estate sector, have transformed what I consider to be more correct from the point of view of economic policy, and I reflect this in the book.

Before studying in Chicago and the 2008 crisis, I was a passionate supporter of liberal policies. I believed that *laissez-faire*, the "invisible hand" of Adam Smith, was the best way to create wealth in a country; today I believe that countries with markets governed by free competition are the most prosperous, but that the State must play an active role to avoid the crises which occur in the economy as a result of the changes in the psychology or opinion of its consumers, of excessive supply or deficits in demand. Crises are inevitable; they have always existed and will always exist. That is

---

[1] John Kenneth Galbraith: "A short history of financial euphoria" and the Crash of 1929". Spanish version by Ariel, a label of Editorial Planeta, S.A.

why it is important to know how to combat them, what measures to take, and why.

There is currently very good literature on the "sub-prime" crisis, and here I would like to focus more on the case of Spain. But I recommend to my readers Paul Krugman's book "End this Depression Now!"[2], as I share the majority of his comments on economic policy to emerge from the current crisis in a fair way and substantially reducing levels of unemployment.

Also for lovers of Economics, I recommend Shiller's book "Animal Spirits"[3] for an understanding of people's behaviour and its impact on economic cycles. Neither should we forget the literature on *"behavioural Economics"*, Richard Thaler and his "Nudge"[4], which explains very clearly this new current on the behaviour of people, of the *homo economicus*. Raghuram Rajan has recently written a very interesting book on the crisis called "Fault lines: how hidden fractures still threaten the world economy"[5], which is well worth reading.

In this crisis monetary policies have been very important; in fact, in some countries, they were the only countercyclical policies.

---

[2] Paul Krugman: "End this depression now!". Spanish version published by Editorial Crítica, S.L.

[3] Robert J Shiller and George A. Akerlof: "Animal spirits". Ediciones Gestión 2000, 2009

[4] Richard Thaler: "Nudge". English version published by Penguin Books.

[5] Raghuram Rajan: "Fault lines: how hidden fractures still threaten the world economy" Published in Spanish by Editorial Deusto SA Ediciones, 2011

The experience of the "Great Depression", studied in particular by Milton Friedman in his "Monetary History of the United States", and the ideas he contributed, prevented the crisis from being even more serious.

Also, the currents of market efficiency and the fact that *homo economicus* is a rational being or has rational expectations is a good lesson in learning what happens in the economy in the long term. Proof of this is the evolution of economies like the US, English, Australian, Canadian and South African economies, where the free market has achieved greater levels of prosperity than in the rest of the world. But the free market does not mean that the State cannot exercise some kind of moderation over economic cycles. As Krugman correctly states, Keynesian policies are not socialist (or, as we understand it in Spain, communist) economic planning policies. We are not talking about five-year plans in the style of the Soviet Union. They are policies and regulation to avoid economic crises such as the Crash of 1929 and the "Second Great Depression" of 2008. This is why John Maynard Keynes' book called "General theory of employment, interest and money"[6] is compulsory reading for anyone interested in the economic policies

---

[6] John Maynard Keynes. Editorial Fondo de Cultura económica de España, S.L. 2006.

a State must apply. Keynes was a genius, just like Friedman. His know-how cannot be forgotten and with this book I hope to contribute to it.

Also important is the work of great economists like Robert Lucas and Eugene Fama, who I met at an event at the University of Chicago. His ideas on the efficiency of markets and the rationality of economic subjects are very useful for theoretical economics, and I believe that this efficiency tends to be found to a greater or lesser degree in economies in the long term, which also appears to be the consensus of the majority of economists. I do not believe, however, that raising interest rates, or lowering the price of the debt of peripheral countries during the crisis were a question of efficiency, but rather "animal spirits" panicking.

Meanwhile, John Huizinga, who was my professor in the two subjects I took in Economics at Chicago, taught me that within positive economics the hypotheses of the Keynesian School are usually fulfilled in the short term, and those of the Classical School in the long term. Experience has shown me that he was probably right. Many of the ideas reflected in this book start from his classes.

What is true is that for Spain, which cannot become indebted in its own currency, resorting to the neo-Keynesian policies which were taught in Spanish universities with Paul Samuelson's book, is very limited. It is why the fiscal expansion plans, such as Plan E, ended up pitting the country against its creditors. Let's not forget that in this crisis Germany has been judge and jury. It has represented the creditors, German savers, and not the citizens who are unemployed in the countries incorrectly considered to be peripheral.

I ask the reader to "listen" to this book, without prejudice, and read it while listening to the arguments. Without anger. Without a preconceived opinion of what is said in it. I want the reader to consider the subject matter and the ideas respectfully, because if we are to prosper we need respectful debate, something which is in regrettably short supply in Spain. Positions have become entrenched and we are lacking a more open mentality to improve. I also ask the reader to look for rationality, to listen to my arguments and think about the topic. In short, I want my reader to have, as English speakers would say, an open mind.

Introduction

The economic crisis does not originate in a financial crisis in which the maximum exponents are American sub-prime mortgages. The crisis occurred fundamentally because the World Economy had very high levels of growth in the second half of the 1990s and post-2003. This is almost certainly because the productivity of work has been sufficiently high to allow growth without generating too much inflation. In the end, even if excessive inflation is not generated in the shopping basket, when there is a very long cycle, inflation occurs in those sectors where production is more rigid and which cannot adapt so quickly to growth. This is what has happened with the real estate sector. The speed at which land is reclassified and housing built is much lower than that which a strongly expanding economy might demand.

Economic growth has generated considerable imbalances, where the lack of supply in the first phase of the cycle in some sectors, such as the real estate sector, has caused prices to increase considerably, thus generating a bubble which subsequently burst.

The phenomenon of economic cycles is well known. In the first stage, demand is not very high and neither is supply; in the second stage, demand increases and supply is not sufficient to meet it, thus creating an upturn in prices, an increase in company profits and the generation of employment to increase supply. In a third phase, thanks to the profits obtained with higher prices, supply increases and demand goes up; a result of this is that new jobs are created, prices go up, and when demand begins to stabilise and supply continues to grow, prices stop rising. Finally, demand decreases, supply continues to increase and this excess supply causes prices to fall, companies start to lose money and have to reduce their excess capacity by firing employees. This, in turn, causes demand to contract even further, leading to a recession.

This is the position Spain was in between 2008 and 2013: after excess production or oversupply, we get a crisis. The greater the excess, the greater the crisis. And the phenomenon occurs again in the opposite direction to emerge from the crisis. Supply contracts, demand reaches a moment when it stabilises, the existing offer of stock is liquidated and once again we need to produce more to satisfy demand. New people are hired again, which generates more demand and so we return to the start of another economic cycle. At school, I remember studying the concept of overproduction in relation to the Crash of 1929. Basically this is what happens in major crises and especially if the financial sector is also affected.

This phenomenon has occurred on numerous occasions and the magnitude of the correction in times of crisis depends on the excess supply generated, which is usually greater if the economic cycle has been longer and companies have earned more money; in turn, they have reinvested in producing more and hiring more people, or when the financial economy is affected in such a way that it affects credit and reduces supply and demand in particular. This is a vicious circle which occurs first with growth and subsequently with contraction.

The causes of the end of the expansion period can be of different types. Usually we look for a specific cause to justify why the cycle, or the bubble, has burst; we usually refer to a bubble when growth has been so high that prices have spiralled out of control. The cause of this crisis was attributed to the sub-prime mortgages and the collapse of Lehman Brothers, but the truth is that the bubble began to burst when, in the spring of 2006, housing prices began to fall in the United States, almost certainly because of the excess supply and because prices had gone up so much that part of the demand preferred to wait. The same thing happened in Spain more or less around the same period in 2007. One year later. We were beginning to produce more than we were selling. The end of the cycle was near.

This time, the crisis has had a very considerable impact on the real estate sector because this was one of the sectors where there was most overheating, and a greater inflation in prices.

Surprisingly, it appears that neither the United States Federal Reserve nor the European Central Bank took rising house prices into account when fixing their monetary policies. This is somewhat curious because the majority of bank guarantees are mortgages. Excessive growth in the price of housing makes corrections more feasible and, consequently, there is a greater risk for a country's financial system. Unfortunately, we have already experienced this phenomenon in previous crises and it would be a good idea for central banks to take particular account of the evolution of house prices when fixing their monetary policies.

Traditionally, central banks have focused on the Consumer Price Index (CPI) or on underlying inflation which excludes some more volatile items such as the price of energy. But the inflation which was occurring in real estate assets had a double influence on the wealth of families and on the stability of the financial system. It is a mistake to fix monetary policy without taking into account that housing has double-digit growth, because sooner or later that will have an effect on domestic economies and on the financial sector.

Why is housing the principal collateral or guarantee for banks? Houses have many advantages as guarantees. In addition to the value of the land on which they are built and their durability, they have the advantage that they do not often decrease much in price.

Why do they not decrease much in price? Fundamentally because they are produced in a sector in which, when there is a crisis, production is drastically reduced, either because it is not necessary to continue producing or because of the lack of bank financing. In a normal industrial sector, a fixed cost is incurred when building a factory, and when the crisis arrives the factory is still there and we have to produce to pay off the cost of construction. Sometimes in the industrial sector there is production at a loss simply to cover the variable costs (workforce, electricity, etc.) and part of the fixed costs (depreciation of the plant). If it is necessary to reduce the price to continue amortizing part of the fixed costs, then it is reduced; the issue here is selling to be able to cover the depreciation and not having to close. This type of companies, such as car manufacturers, know that they are losing money when times are hard but that they will earn money when times are good. They like this idea because although they lose money, chances are they will earn more and compensate for the loss in the future.

In addition, because part of the amortization costs of industrial plants are not genuine outgoings, sometimes they operate with positive cash flows despite having losses in the profit and loss account. Sometimes this is not the case because they are paying for the financing which was necessary to buy the factory or the land on which it is built. In this case, it is also necessary to continue operating to cover these fixed costs.

In the real estate sector there is no factory. There is land paid for with own financing (equity) or partly with financing from elsewhere (debt). In the first case, production is substantially reduced during the crisis, and some companies which are self financing, which are a minority, either do not produce or reduce their production substantially so as not to lose liquidity. In the second case, the bank does not want to finance the project unless the company is very solvent and the land is in a place where there is no excess supply. Sometimes, when the company which owned the land has suspended payments or is bankrupt, the bank takes the land and after a number of years decides either to develop it or sell it so that someone else can develop it. A common feature of this crisis has been for banks to look for developers or constructors to develop land which they have recovered, in good locations, sharing the risk. The bank provides the land and the developer buys it when a considerable part of the development is already sold. In addition, the bank usually helps with selling. At that point, the bank begins to finance so that the project can be finished and the houses can be sold. Buyers finally take over the developer's mortgage, which is divided for each client, or clients cancel the mortgage by paying it off.

But this is an exception, because residential real estate production during crises falls considerably. Applications for new building permits in Spain fell by up to 90% and more compared to maximum values. Little by little stock is being exhausted. Housing prices stabilise depending on the magnitude of the crisis. In our case, this is very high because the appropriate fiscal policies were not adopted, and there was no possibility of devaluing the currency because we are part of the Euro.

From the figures in the book "This time is different: Eight centuries of financial folly" by Kenneth S Rogoff and Carmen M Reinhart[7], we can talk about an average of five years of falling prices in real estate crises (if we exclude the Japanese crisis). In this crisis, the fall in the United States lasted more or less that time. In

---

[7] Kenneth S. Rogoff y Carmen M. Reinhart, "This time is different: Eight centuries of financial folly". Spanish version: Fondo de Cultura Económica de España, S.L, 2011

Spain we are talking about seven years or so, fundamentally because of joining the Euro. Added to the usual crisis, we have a crisis of external solvency and liquidity, which required an internal devaluation and which, in this case because it could not be via a monetary devaluation, has taken place slowly through a devaluation of real salaries and the value of assets compared to overseas, including real estate assets.

In addition, real estate assets usually have great durability and their value does not depreciate over time like other assets, such as a car. In the long term, houses are usually worth more (provided we have inflation). This is what is known in Microeconomics as a costs increasing industry, where the long-term value of land tends to go up.

Why have prices fallen by more than 30% in this crisis? Fundamentally because excess production has been so high because of large price increases that it is normal for a correction to occur. Furthermore, the devaluation of salaries in real terms has not been carried out by creating inflation by devaluing the exchange rate; because Spain is in the Euro, it does not control its monetary policy. This was something it was able to do in the crisis of 1992.

Before the crisis, the economy was growing strongly without generating inflation and the central banks had very low reference rates, which allowed mortgages which were excessively cheap for the real situation of the economy.

Even so, house prices have still not fallen below the levels for 2000 and they are unlikely to do so. Currently, in mid-2015, prices are at levels close to those of the beginning of 2002. And they are still very much above the levels of the 1990s. In real terms (excluding inflation), they are even below those of the mid 1990s. This is a frequent phenomenon: when crises arrive, the housing market adjusts, prices return in real terms to more or less those of the previous decade, and the financial effort required to buy a house returns more or less to the previous average. This adjustment in previous crises occurred in terms relative to other economies thanks to the decrease in the peseta; in this crisis housing prices has gone down directly in Euros. This is why the drop is more appreciable for Spanish people than when their currency was devalued, but it is equally an adjustment in the value of salaries and assets. The difference is in time. The crisis at the beginning of the 1990s was resolved with a monetary devaluation and it was much shorter than the current one.

Overproduction during the boom periods in the economic cycle is not just in the real estate sector, which is a very pro-cyclical sector, but rather it is overproduction which has occurred in the economy in general, and particularly in those sectors which are more dependent on domestic demand, which was tremendously strong during the economic boom. In Spain, this boom lasted from the crisis at the beginning of the 1990s until more or less 2008. Here the crisis of 2000-2001 was felt very little. This boom did not come about by accident, and behind it, in addition to components of excess liquidity, there were others of a more fundamental nature. During these years, people born during the *baby boom* became part of the Working Population, the impact of improved worker training was felt, education became more generalised and women entered the employment market. These are just a few of the reasons.

From 2003 to 2008 there was an increase in production factors, and their productivity, leading to an increase in production which was then sold; this affected demand, in turn generated more employment and, consequently, even more growth in domestic demand. If we add to this the fact that it was also easy to obtain financing from overseas, thanks to joining the Monetary Union, we had all the elements for the economy to grow, especially investment in residential property.

In Spain, and the other countries incorrectly called peripheral or Southern European, the cost of financing went down when we joined the Euro. The risk for European savers of investing in a peripheral country in the Euro zone decreased, as they could invest in buying bonds in any country of the Euro zone in their own currency, with the European Central Bank guaranteeing price stability.

The problem arose when the ECB, which was focusing only on underlying inflation and was worried about weak growth in Germany, which was carrying out reforms which affected its economy, implemented a very lax monetary policy which led to real short-term interest rates in Spain and other peripheral countries becoming negative. This added to the leverage of families and companies and made the bubble even bigger. The ECB did not act correctly, and neither did the Federal Reserve. Low inflation rates appeared to demand this monetary policy, but increasing property and raw material prices indicated that the world economy was overheating.

During the crisis the ECB performed worse than other central banks because it raised reference rates twice at times when it should not have done so. It raised rates too soon, committing the same mistake as Greenspan had done in 1994. Trichet's management was very poor.

Fortunately, he was replaced by Mario Draghi, who has demonstrated a greater ability to solve problems, though not without difficulties. Even so, subsequent analysis shows that his efforts were late and not sufficiently intense. Almost certainly because the fiscal policies are contractionary, which is somewhat surprising at a time when private domestic demand in countries is contracting.

The Spanish government of José Luis Rodriguez Zapatero also could have done more, and should have applied a restrictive fiscal policy before the crisis to slow down the bubble and thus prevent the subsequent crisis from being as serious as it eventually was. If the problem was one of private debt, surely the most appropriate move would have been to raise taxes. For example, they could have increased VAT on house purchases or have removed the deduction for house purchases. These were unpopular measures which the government would have felt at the following elections. Unfortunately, these measures were taken later during the real estate crisis, when obliged to do so by Brussels, and at that time they made the fall in house prices even worse.

Perhaps the Spanish Socialist Party (PSOE) would have won the 2008 elections less convincingly, but surely it would not have lost the 2011 elections in such a calamitous fashion. In the end, public intervention is justified to temper the economic cycle and to ensure there is greater fairness between all citizens. It would have been the perfect time to remember Keynes, who is usually only remembered when we are already in a crisis and not before.

It could be argued that the country had a fiscal surplus in the years running up to the crisis, but it is obvious that it was not sufficient. Much more could have been done to prevent what happened and the reading is that we have to learn from it. When the economy returns to employment levels similar to those of 2007, which are surely those of full employment in Spain, measures must be taken to generate the fiscal surplus which will allow increased public spending in future times of crisis. How can this increase be carried out? The answer is very easy: by increasing public spending in areas which generate more value for the economy in the future: public investment in education, research and necessary and profitable infrastructures.

It is fundamental here to criticise the Government of the time, not for whether it predicted the possibility of a crisis, but for failing to take effective action when faced with the bubble. What were needed were countercyclical measures which in the short and medium term, to a certain degree, would have slowed down the excess demand being fed by excessively cheap financing for the real risk which was being incurred.

For this reason, in the future it would be desirable for governments to take into account what is happening in the real estate sector when evaluating which point in the economic cycle we are at, and what impact it might have in the future on the country's economy and public finances. It is true that this criticism could be levelled at the majority of governments in countries which suffered from the crisis, and it is easy to do so after the event. Whatever the case, we must remember this for the following cycle, and I hope this book contributes to that. History always repeats itself, although the details may differ.

In the case of Spain, it would be appropriate to criticise the public management of the Savings Banks (*Cajas de Ahorros*). Their management did not take into account that the economy is cyclical and that financing land is a very dangerous thing. In order to capture the end customer buying a house, and sell them a mortgage, insurance, etc., the financial institutions began to finance real estate developments which gave them easy customers. Subsequently, as the competition increased, they began to finance land to capture real estate developers or the manager of cooperatives which would build the development and provide them with their customers. This financing of land, which reached 80% of the value of the land, is high-risk financing because land is an asset with very little liquidity and its price can be highly volatile, something which was shown subsequently when the bubble burst.

The public Savings Banks behaved worse than the private banks, fundamentally because they had different incentives. Whereas banks were controlled to a certain degree by their majority shareholders, in the Savings Banks there were insufficient controls over their governing bodies, which had a greater tendency to defend their own interests – as can be seen in the different cases of corruption which have come to light subsequently – rather than those of the taxpayer.

Both BBVA bank and Santander bank, together with Banco Sabadell, Bankinter and the Banco Popular, have shown that private management in Spain was much better than public management in this crisis. This may be due to the fact that their managers had experience of previous crises and because they saw how the market was starting to have problems in the United States before Spain, which allowed them to prepare themselves. We should not, however, forget that during this crisis many private international entities have had to be rescued by their Governments or have experienced serious problems: it is calculated that between 2008 and 2011 in the United States alone more than 400 banks received funds or were "bailed out".

However, as we will discuss later on, the consolidation of the Spanish financial system may bring serious problems for future crises. The idea of being "too big to fail" is a phenomenon discussed in the English-speaking world, but which has not been sufficiently debated in Spain for our financial system. The concentration of the Spanish financial system is not positive for the long term and brings with it considerable risks for the next cycle. A similar problem to the one which countries like the United Kingdom and France will have.

Chapter 1: the real estate crash

As I mentioned earlier, the principal reason for the intensity of the economic crisis in Spain, and in the countries incorrectly called "peripheral", is their entry into the Euro. When the countries in southern Europe joined Monetary Union, the risk premiums demanded for financing families and companies had to be drastically reduced compared to the countries of northern Europe. The new reality that behind these countries would be the solvency of a Central Bank like the ECB and a currency like the Euro meant that the perception of risk was lower, and consequently the cost of financing was reduced considerably. At that time, an investor from northern Europe could invest in southern European bonds, earning more interest and in his own currency, with the added incentive that as the *spreads* were reduced, with the convergence of interest rates, he would earn even more.

We might say that the same thing happened with the United States sub-prime crisis: those families less able to pay their loans received a larger quantity of credit and in better conditions than they should have received if there hadn't been as much liquidity and, above all, so much propensity for risk deriving from a very long expansive economic cycle. In the United States there is a tendency to attribute this blame to Congress, which is accused of making the conditions for granting loans much more flexible for the less advantaged classes. I believe, as Krugman does, that this is a mistake. The truth is that the duration of the economic cycle and an excessively lax monetary policy stimulated credit. The US government should have introduced countercyclical policies to slow down expansion a little and limit the risks; for its part, the Federal Reserve (Fed) should have raised interest rates earlier to slow down the rise in house prices.

On the old continent, the capacity for payment in the southern countries was limited by trade balances and more credit entered then they would be able to pay in the future. The best example of this is Greece, a relatively small country with a very large deficit in its trade balance. The overseas dependence of these economies was a factor which worsened the public debt crisis.

Countries with a greater overseas deficit and which shared a common currency have suffered this to a greater extent.

In the years prior to the real estate boom, while Germany was being reunified and attempting to emerge from the stagnation of the start of the century, the ECB reduced interest rates to facilitate the adjustment being carried out by the Germans with low inflation rates; at that time Spanish citizens could obtain financing at negative real rates. Logically, this was an incentive for private individuals to invest by requesting loans, and this is what they did. Soon, housing prices rocketed with purchases leveraged by mortgage loans and nobody put a brake on it. Neither Greenspan nor Trichet seemed particularly interested in slowing down the rise in real estate prices. The cost of living reflected by the CPI in housing is measured in terms of monthly spending on rent but not in terms of mortgages. Insufficient attention was paid to the effect that the rise in house prices had on the wealth of families and their financial solvency, or on the effects a sharp fall in these prices would have.

Back in 2005 there were economists who were warning of the rise in house prices and raw materials, and the risks this would have in the medium and long term. House prices continued to rise and rise, and this was an incentive to buy quickly because if you didn't you could be left out of the market. But, as with all bubbles,

40

one day they have to burst. The cause is attributed to the American sub-prime mortgages and the collapse of Lehman Brothers but housing, as we have already said, had already started to fall in the United States in the spring of 2006, and in Spain in the spring of 2007. As soon as the central banks raised rates in 2008 to slow down rising inflation, they worsened the fall in house prices. Soon the trend would be inverted. The bubble had burst. Housing prices began to fall, defaults in payments began to increase, and housing developments were not selling as they were before. Construction companies and housing developers began to fire employees, consumer demand fell, companies producing the goods they consumed began to fire their employees who, in turn, consumed less, and the economic cycle took a downturn. The vicious circle of falling demand which feeds itself.

Sales of housing with a purchase or pre-sale contract began to slow down in 2007, but the real effects were felt in 2008 when the ECB's reference interest rates rose and the Euribor rate at one year increased by more than 5.5%. This rise was an example of what you should not do in monetary policy. The ECB had not noticed the fall in house prices in the United States in 2006 which was also starting to happen in Europe. Nobody noticed the Case-Shiller index or the equivalent indices in European economies, because the obsession was with inflation, including the price of raw materials, which was now out of control because of an economic overheating which should have been stopped much earlier.

For a mortgage granted in 2003, in 2008, after the ECB's rise and its impact on the Euribor at one year rate, buyers had to pay double the monthly amount they were paying five years earlier. The housing market came to an abrupt halt. Sales disappeared overnight.

There were still good figures for prior pre-sales which meant that in 2008 the number of title deeds did not fall as much as pre-sales. But in reality the market had dried up. There was no demand. As many operations failed as new ones were created. In 2008 very few houses were sold. It was the warning that a big storm was coming.

With "Plan E" approved, the fiscal stimulus was soon noted by the spring of 2009, and the market took a slight upturn. Properties began to be sold and 2009 was a bad year but not a catastrophic one. However, public deficit problems soon arrived. The fiscal stimulus was very positive on the demand side but it did not generate sufficient growth to pay for its cost, and behind it there was no possibility of financing it with the central bank itself (providing the necessary liquidity to invest in state debt and devaluing the currency, in order to attract overseas capital to finance the cost and, in turn, increase exports, which also generates capital). And so we would suffer during 2010, made worse by the fact that we had an economy with a negative trade balance which needed overseas financing, as was the case with Spain.

As public finances continued to deteriorate, the result of receding private demand and a public sector which was trying to stimulate the economy in fiscal terms but was not able to do so, creditors began to believe that the State would not be able to pay their debt. When it comes to paying debts, it is much more catastrophic for a State to have unemployment of 25% than having to withstand 10% deficit for two or three years. This is an overreaction which happens in the short term when faced with financial crises: as the Nobel prize-winner Shiller would say, using Keynes terminology, we are "animal spirits". The fact that private citizens were highly indebted was a bad presentation letter to give to creditors who were financing Spain.

In real terms, private debt seemed high whereas public debt did not. It made no sense to radically reduce the deficit because, on the one hand, it stimulated domestic demand in the economy by reducing unemployment and, on the other, it transformed private debt into public debt, the cost of which is lower for citizens as a whole. In July 2015 it was estimated that, since the start of the crisis, private debt had fallen by 40% of GDP whereas public debt had grown by 60%. The interest in reducing the deficit was a matter for creditors, who in this case were led by Germany and its citizens. A greater fiscal stimulus, as Paul Krugman suggests in his book on the crisis, would have been useful in reducing levels of unemployment, stabilising the economy and making the total debt, both public and private, more sustainable.

A country's economy does not work in the same way as a private economy: if you reduce spending, this has an impact on your own domestic demand and with it you also reduce GDP in the short term. With an appropriate stimulus in public spending the crisis could have been reduced substantially and the creditors would also have come out on top, as monetary policy would not have to have been so lax and interest rates would not have decreased so much. We have contributed to the loss of demand with our "austerity" policies, reducing public spending and increasing taxes, and we have generated deflation, which has meant that monetary policy has had to do all the work. We have fallen into the "liquidity trap" which Keynes spoke about, and which was also described by John Hicks using the IS-LM model, and have done nothing to get out of it.

The ECB had to perform Quantitative Easing, like the US Federal Reserve, with extremely low rates to stimulate monetary supply, but we could have done more by increasing public spending at the same time. The monetary policy would not have needed to be so aggressive, unemployment would certainly have been less in the countries of southern Europe, as would their idle capacity, and both debtors and creditors would have come out winning. But fear is free. We have bond investors buying long-term public debt at ridiculous prices with yields inferior to the inflation which will exist in the future, because there is excessive saving caused by excessive fear; and we have inoperative States which could have solved this problem from the outset.

Thanks to the Federal Reserve, we have not ended up with an insufficient money supply which causes deflation, as happened in the Japanese crisis. The ECB replicated the policy adopted by the Fed, more or less late. We have to thank Milton Friedman and his "Monetary History of the United States": without his explanations of the Great Depression, monetary policy today would have been less aggressive and more unsatisfactory. Let's not forget that an increase in the money supply, which is increased by raising the monetary base or reducing the requirements for reserves, does not increase production in the long term. This is why reducing unemployment is not an ECB objective; its only fundamental objective is price stability (equal to or close to 2% annual inflation).

But I will go further than this. During 2009, I had the opportunity to talk to a number of foreigners about the crisis in Spain and the real estate sector. All of them had a more negative perception than what was actually happening. It was in 2010, when pressures to reduce public deficits began, that the real crisis started. There was a crisis in 2008 from which we were emerging in 2009 with fiscal stimuli. But soon Germany and Angela Merkel's new austerity policies worsened the problems throughout Europe. The mistaken policies of increasing taxes and reducing spending which Herbert Hoover had applied in the United States during the crash of 1929 were now being applied in Europe. It seemed like History had forgotten Roosevelt's New Deal and the influence that John Maynard Keynes had had on Economic Science.

Obama's administration did better, but his stimulus plan was clearly insufficient.

The Spanish state issued its debt in Euros without the support of a Central Bank which could buy it. Soon, liquidity problems appeared. Investors' money, including Spanish investors, was going to countries with more positive trade balances, a smaller public deficit and which were also perceived as being more solvent. In this case Germany was the great beneficiary of fear. The remaining peripheral economies were left with no liquidity.

In order to rescue these countries (given that the ECB at that time was not buying debt to provide liquidity in the secondary market), Germany and the creditor countries erroneously demanded austerity measures, like those you would demand of a private citizen when he or she cannot pay his debts. This forced the Spanish government, in July 2010, to raise VAT to reduce public deficit. This is where the second crisis began. These measures, like those of Herbert Hoover, made the problem worse.

The situation was absurd. If we compare Spain's public debt now as a percentage of GDP with a private economy, we are saying that if said debt is approximately 100% of its annual GDP, then a private citizen earning €30,000 a year, in other words €2500 a month, would have a debt of €30,000. For lovers of this type of comparisons with their own family economy: does this seem excessive to you? In fact, the Chicago Booth professor John Huizinga showed us that calculating an average taxation of 20% of an economy's GDP, and with the political will to pay off the debt (something which did not happen in Argentina, for example) we could withstand theoretical debts of up to 500% of GDP. If this is the case then why does it not happen in reality? Because people are free to panic and because doubts always arise about whether a government is prepared to demand sufficient taxes from its citizens to pay off that debt. Rogoff and Reinhart's figures about how debt of more than 90% affects an economy's growth are more than debatable.

Using figures from 2012 and 2013, Germany's foreign debt was 142%, Spain's was 167% and the United Kingdom's was 406%. In other words, the situation in Spain was not as bad as everyone was saying.

Between December 2009 and May 2010 the real estate market stabilised to a certain degree in sales, although not in prices (although we are talking here about official statistics, because the real price figures are much more volatile than those that appear in the statistics), both because of fiscal expansion and because of the announcement of tax increases which obliged many house-hunters to bring forward their purchases. House sales stabilised, or went up slightly, and even reached the point where they were more or less normal if we do not consider the boom years as being normal.

After July 2010 however, the effect of the fiscal contraction which involved an increase in VAT on housing right in the middle of falling prices (a surprising pro-cyclical measure), the tendency to disinvest and de-leverage, as well as the effect that the destruction of employment was starting to have on demand, meant that sales fell radically during that year. The end of 2010 was bad, but not as bad as 2011, 2012 and 2013 would be. 2013 will be remembered as the worst year in the Spanish real estate sector in a long time.

In 2011, the real estate market had practically disappeared. House purchases represented approximately 10% of those registered in the boom years. We had reached the sector's wilderness years. At the end of the year the government announced a 4% decrease in VAT, which stimulated the market to a certain extent, although the news that the possible future government of Mariano Rajoy, if it won the elections, would extend this measure in 2012, meant that sales did not increase substantially.

2012 started badly, because buyers had brought forward the purchase of houses, but catastrophe came when the decrees issued by the new economics minister, Luis de Guindos, (commonly known as the De Guindos decrees) were approved. The idea behind these was to oblige banks to make more radical provisions for real estate. This was a nuclear bomb in the real estate sector. At that moment the banks started to sell off the real estate. Developers' sales disappeared completely. Many opted for renting with an option to buy. This was a solution which some companies had started to use in the first years of the crisis and which, with the considerable drop in prices, was not the best solution.

Because of the lack of monetary policy mechanisms – the currency could not be devalued because we were in the Euro – and being unable to increase domestic demand with a greater fiscal stimulus because of lack of money, Spain opted to attract overseas capital to stop the crisis getting any worse, in the form of equity from international real estate investment funds (first vultures and opportunists, and then core and value-added funds). Luis de Guindos, I believe seeing the evils which had converted the Japanese crisis into a structural one, and comparing them with the situation at that time in Spain, promoted these decrees which, although they were very bad for the financial and real estate sectors, stimulated the liquidation of stocks and the entry of foreign capital. It was making the crisis worse in an attempt to emerge from it with overseas financing. It was avoiding having an economy with zombie banks which could not give credit because their balance sheets contained a large amount of assets in unaccounted losses. One way of bringing an end to a crisis is to force it even further down in an attempt to find the market floor. The regulations on Real Estate Investment Trusts (REIT) were also modified with major tax breaks for international investors.

Soon we would see the crisis at Bankia which, obliged to make provisions, needed impressive recapitalisation if it was to carry on operating. This was a bank with almost 300 billion in assets at the end of 2011, representing 30% of Spanish GDP. From that moment on, banks sold off their real estate, giving preferential financing conditions (very often 100%) to house buyers. The obligatory provisions of the "De Guindos Decrees" had meant that, even when selling below the market price, the bank would give profits on what had already been provided for. It forced the market price down even further. Housing prices collapsed by more than 10% that year in year-on-year terms.

Whereas in the United States Bernanke was trying to influence Americans' expectations of inflation with Quantitative Easings, with the fundamental objective of stabilising house prices – which is the principal guarantee of the banks – in Spain De Guindos was bringing out a decree which was being sold as a way of offering transparency to international investors, but which in fact only managed to collapse the domestic market. Precipitating house prices causes the banks to lose guarantees, and increases the default rates of both developers and private individuals: reducing people's wealth to reduce the duration of the crisis. Put an end to the crisis by making it worse.

As if that was not enough, De Guindos stated that his objective was to bring down house prices and that they were going to come down even more. In this way he achieved just the opposite of what Bernanke was trying to achieve: expectations of deflation. These expectations clearly reduce investment, in this case residential investment in the purchase of houses, and contribute to recession.

When you collapse the domestic market imports decrease, domestic companies which can export do what they can to sell overseas because they are unable to sell their products domestically, and we end up with a trade surplus. This is good because it reduces your need for external financing, and you solve the real problem of the Spanish economy, which is external dependence with a currency not controlled domestically; however, it is bad for those who have businesses in Spain, which are the majority, which see their profits fall and end up making cost cuts and cuts in their workforce. Short-term unemployment increases, as does general unease. This would have its impact on the way the government was valued and on the boom in new political parties, some of them with a communist ideology. This unease would be a millstone around the Government's neck at the 2015 regional and municipal elections.

Domestic demand decreases so much that unemployment goes up and this cannot be offset with increased activity and demand for labour generated by exports; hence the economy continues to fall, the unemployed consume less and necessary domestic production is lower. We are now in the crisis at the end of 2012 and 2013. Although by the end of 2013 the economy would grow thanks to increased exports, the domestic market and the residential investment market were still depressed. It began to recover in 2014 and 2015 but on a very low base.

With regard to the necessary internal devaluation of salaries made easier by employment reform, in a simple IS-LM macro economic model real salaries are usually used as an adjustment variable, but such models simplify reality. A reduction in the value of land and houses, offices, etc. causes the economy to adjust and it becomes more interesting for a foreigner to invest in Spain or even for a Spaniard who has liquidity to begin to invest. In other words, the fall in real estate assets contributes positively to this increased competitiveness, which also comes with a slight reduction in salaries, which as we know, is a much more inflexible market.

The first people to put a floor on the market are the investors, which is why a very large percentage of the sales selling off houses from the banks' balance sheets have been in cash and without financing. This is why the people who have bought are investors who have liquidity. Then the rest of the people looking for housing will buy as credit becomes normalised (let's not forget that this credit also comes from investors who gain confidence and begin to lend it).

We have had a crisis with falls in housing prices since 2007, more than seven years. This period is longer than a usual real estate crisis, which tends to last about five years. The fact that the adjustment has been slower is due to our entry into the Euro.

54

Chapter 2: the Euro and the unemployment problem

When the Spanish joined the Euro it was never explained to them that this meant an end to the mechanism of devaluing the exchange rate as an instrument for competitive adjustment of the country's economy during times of crisis. If we had not been in the Euro, devaluation would have meant that the economy recovered sooner thanks to an increase in exports and a reduction in imports (to the detriment of those who had wealth accumulated in Euros, which is restated in the new currency). This recovery of exports would have occurred earlier because, amongst other factors, relative real salaries compared to other currencies would have fallen. In addition, investment would also have recovered earlier because assets in the new devalued currency would be cheaper for international investors. Imports would have fallen substantially because they were more expensive, improving the economy's trade balance.

Credit markets would have financed us earlier without "austerity" because new investors would have seen that our currency is highly devalued and with the new higher rates with a devalued currency investment appetite would have returned.

A 40% devaluation would have prevented domestic house prices from falling in the local currency, although in relative terms citizens would have become poorer compared to other Europeans. Being in the Euro means (with no possibility for a fiscal stimulus – like the one being tried now with the "Juncker plan") that the adjustment is slower and must involve a reduction in salaries or an increase in prices, i.e. inflation. Because the ECB has a 2% inflation objective, the adjustment must come primarily from a fall in salaries.

And that is what happened: the adjustment came about by reducing the economy's total salaries, fundamentally through unemployment, which has reached almost 27% of the active population. One of the reasons why the adjustment has been through employment and not so much from employees' salaries has been the lack of flexibility of the employment market. Fortunately, the Popular Party government made the employment market more flexible, which allowed fewer jobs to be destroyed in exchange for a reduction in salaries. Logically, because the employment market is not a very flexible market, this reduction in salaries is slow even when employment legislation becomes more flexible.

In my opinion, however, the inflexibility of the employment market has not been the fundamental reason for the high level of unemployment. The fundamental reason is related to the type of activity which occurs in our economy. Construction and the restaurant and hotel trades are very intensive businesses with a workforce with very low added value. When there is a fall in sales this is soon followed not only by losses but also reductions in cash flow, and the workforce has to be reduced because it is the principle cost which reduces cash flow at that time. It is not like a luxury car factory. If you have already paid for the production plant and amortised part of it and sales fall, your workforce continues to be an important cost which drains cash flow, but your treasury is not reduced so much because it generates income which allows you to cover that variable workforce cost and part of the fixed cost of amortising the investment in the factory. Once you have paid for your factory or paid off part of the loan on it, if your business has a high added value it takes time until your sales are reduced so much that the workforce drains so much liquidity from the business that you have to close. But if you have a bar, and overnight 20% of your tables remain empty, soon you will have too many waiters or you begin to reduce your liquidity. Depending on whether the type of activity has a greater or lesser added value, and whether it is more or less financed, with greater or lesser debt servicing, it affects how your cash flow is reduced during the crisis.

The residential sales real estate business has both of these problems: it is only of great added value when the price rises considerably because of lack of supply, but that value goes to the increase in value of future lands necessary to continue with the activity. Furthermore, it is usually highly leveraged, which means that it needs considerable debt servicing and also needs to amortise the capital with a certain speed, provided it is the developer who is paying because the houses have not been sold.

If you add to this the fact that the residential real estate business is cyclical and that sales can fall overnight, soon you have a domino effect in the whole economy, where the principle incentive is to fire people, and as demand decreases further, more people are fired.

This means that unemployment in Greece or Spain, which are more focused on services and on tourism with low added value, is greater than in Germany or Japan, where industrial activity with high added value represents a larger part of the economy. On top of that, however, Greece is a country which is very dependent on foreign capital because it is small and very tourist-oriented. When crises arrive in the Euro zone, the capital from the Central European countries which have a trade surplus soon starts to panic and wants to return home. Germany, Holland, etc. are conservative countries with lower consumption and more savings. They are the ones which have the money. When fear arrives, money flies away from the peripheral countries, starting with the smallest ones which depend most on overseas. Greece, Iceland, Cyprus, then panic increases, Ireland, Portugal, Spain, Italy and finally France. The contagion spreads everywhere. When the financial crisis arrives money wants to return to its country and someone who has something saved up in the peripheral countries also wants to take it to a safe haven.

Max Weber explained these patterns of saving and consumption in terms of customs related to religious beliefs. In the Protestant countries the economy grows more because of the accumulation of capital and greater technical work because religion has created a culture, or has at least influenced it, in which people can go to heaven if they are austere, hard-working and serious, and simply praying is not the most important thing. Technical jobs, such as engineers, in the Protestant countries predominate over more humanist jobs, such as lawyers, which are more typical in the Catholic countries. It even explains these differences in the German regions with a greater or lesser Protestant or Catholic population. Furthermore, the determinism with which people were born in these Protestant countries (for example, in Puritanism or Calvinism) demanded that if a person wanted to be "saved", he or she had to have spotless behaviour (at work and paying off debts), compared to the Catholic countries where there is room for repentance and forgiveness. This influence of religion on the culture of countries is obvious. My summary here of Weber's book "The Protestant ethic and the spirit of capitalism"[8], although very unsophisticated, seems to me a very good explanation of why economic development through accumulation of capital has occurred in Protestant countries. I think that the explanation is very accurate and although I have read some authors, such as Luis Garicano, criticise it in his book "Spain's dilemma"[9], I think Max Weber was right and knew his subject very well. The closest thing to this culture of work that we have in the Spanish Catholic world is the Opus Dei doctrine. And it is true that many people associated with this doctrine are serious, very hard-working and have money.

---

[8] Max Weber. "The Protestant ethic and the spirit of capitalism". Ed. Alianza Editorial

[9] Luis Garicano. "El dilema de España". Ed. Península. 2014.

The explanation of nations' wealth expressed in the book "Why nations fail"[10] by Daron Acemoglu and James A. Robinson, does not strike me as complete. It is true that solid institutions are a requirement for generating wealth, but what I don't know is whether sometimes they are the cause or sometimes the effect of the evolution of wealth itself. On the other hand, the fact that the State does not have institutions which extract the wealth of private individuals does appear to me a partial explanation of how this can evolve in the long term. In other words, a more extractive society, such as a communist country, will be poorer than one which is less extractive. But this will not be the only reason; it also depends on the degree of economic freedom of its economy. It is a complicated subject with a difficult explanation. I also think that the geographical location has an indirect effect on the level of wealth in so much as it is not the same living on the border with Central Europe (Catalonia or Slovenia) as living on the border with Africa or the poorest outskirts of Europe (Andalusia or Macedonia).

As regards the phenomenon of the flight of capital towards the richer parts of Europe with positive trade balances, it has happened in this crisis and will happen in subsequent crises, for as

---

[10] Daron Acemoglu and James A. Robinson. "Why nations fail". Ed. Deusto. 2012.

long as there are no Eurobonds. When panic arrives money becomes conservative. It flees from housing, which can collapse, it flees from Greece which is on the brink of ruin, it flees from everything which has a hint of risk. To prevent this we have the European Central Bank and the governments of the European Union. Why? Because it is in everyone's interest for this panic to be as moderate as possible so that the economy does not end up like it has ended up. However, the ECB raised rates twice during the crisis, showing signs that it was not aware of what was happening, and governments requested a reduction in public deficit at a time when this was the only thing supporting their economies. Was there another solution? Certainly the best option for the suffering population of southern Europe was the one taken by the United States, although this means that its economy continues to have a trade deficit and is very dependent on foreign capital.

We have seen examples of how to manage a crisis. The US model, surely inherited from what was learnt from Milton Friedman on monetary policy and Keynes on fiscal matters (applied by Franklin D. Roosevelt in his "New Deal").

Bernanke has performed quite well by influencing the expectations of inflation, especially in the housing market, and the same has happened with Obama and his economic team, who have been able to apply the necessary fiscal stimuli and the measures to help the housing market which were necessary to avoid it bleeding to death. Although, as Krugman rightly points out, this was insufficient and sometimes deficient.

Compared to the US model, we have the European model, which has spread fear and even led to questions whether some countries will remain in the Euro. Merely questioning whether Greece will remain has a negative influence on the whole perception of risk in the Euro zone and contributes to making the situation worse. At the time it was not the Greeks' fault, but now in 2015 feeding this situation is starting to be their fault.

Sometimes in politics we talk about neoclassical economists compared to Keynesian economists. Socialist voters support more the measures taken by Keynesian policies, whereas Christian Democrat voters support neoclassical policies. In Economics it is more or less clear that Keynesians are right in the short term and neoclassicists in the long term. In other words, Keynesians talk about real salaries being adjusted slowly and, consequently, the state has to intervene in crises to reduce their duration. This is obviously true, they are quite right. But on the other hand, the neoclassicists talk about the importance of freedom in the markets and that production resources should be allocated depending on the market and not on the State; it is obvious that capitalist economies function better than socialist (for this read communist) economies, which end up carrying out economic planning and allocating non-productive resources in non-productive sectors.

Perhaps a Keynesian prefers to increase public spending in a situation of crisis rather than reducing taxes. But both measures are stimulus measures in the short term. A neoclassicist prefers to reduce spending and taxes, and for the market to adjust gradually in the medium term. This is what we are doing now in Spain to a certain degree. The problem with this solution is the level of unemployment in the short and medium term. In the long term it is a good solution.

But what about the unemployed? In my opinion, in this crisis the most intelligent thing would have been for the non-peripheral countries, i.e. Germany and those who follow her, to allow more fiscal flexibility or even finance fiscal stimuli at the same time as the ECB reduced interest rates more rapidly and introduced measures to avoid fragmentation in the credit markets. All of this is thinking in the short term. It could have acted earlier and with more determination. That way we would have avoided unemployment levels close to 27%, little by little the economy would have reproduced creative destruction to reallocate resources to the more productive sectors and we would have emerged from the crisis in a fairer manner.

The USA takes measures more aggressively than Europe because, as Raghuram Rajan, the governor of the Central Bank of India and Professor on leave of absence from the business school at the University of Chicago explains very well in his book "Fault Lines: How Hidden Fractures Still Threaten the World Economy", it does not have a social security system which allows a prolonged crisis over time without there being a social crisis. Previously, the risk of a crisis of this type in Europe was smaller thanks to the Welfare State, but forcing the peripheral countries to reduce their public deficit without the initial support of the European Central Bank meant that unemployment continued to increase over a long period and brought with it the incorrectly named "populism". The extreme left is nothing more than a logical reaction to the measures, or lack of them, which have excessively increased unemployment. Europe's objective should have been to reduce this unemployment and not reduce the deficit. The deficit should have been reduced little by little as employment was regenerated.

A problem has been created for the capitalist Economy. Instability has returned because we have lacked measures appropriate to the size of the problem. It appears that we have failed to learn the lessons of the Crash of 1929. In a small crisis we could have been less unequivocal in terms of the reforms required and the fiscal and monetary policies implemented; but in this crisis, which is much larger and perhaps has a certain structural content, although almost certainly much less than that which the markets discounted in the worst years of the crisis, what were necessary were much more aggressive monetary and fiscal stimulus measures.

Monetary-type measures are being applied too late and incorrectly. Too late because they are arriving a long time after than in the case of the Fed. The USA is emerging from the crisis before Europe. For too long we have failed to meet the ECB's inflation target with inflation which is too low (it would have been better to overshoot the target, and even increase the inflation target temporarily to 3%). And incorrectly because the ECB's mandate should have been expanded earlier to allow it to make selective purchases where the problem was greater, which was in mortgages and peripheral debt.

This would have rebalanced markets experiencing problems much sooner and would have contributed substantially to reducing the duration of the crisis and its impact on unemployment. We could have prevented a lot of suffering amongst the most disadvantaged families. From that point, in Spain we should have reduced spending slowly to readjust the deficit in an attempt to generate surplus to reduce debt. This is more or less what is happening now, but we should have implemented a greater stimulus and reduced spending more slowly. Almost certainly the deficit would have been corrected at a similar speed, or not much more slowly, thanks to increased tax revenue from greater economic growth. We would be creating much more employment than we are at the moment, as happened in previous crises where recovery was much quicker and employment was also created more quickly.

But a different route was chosen to emerge from the crisis: reduction of public deficit, but without sufficient monetary stimuli and without fiscal stimuli which had the support of other countries with lower debt. Deficit reduction has not been achieved completely because in the end we have entered a spiral of less growth or shrinkage, less public revenue and more unemployment.

This model for emerging from the crisis which we have applied in Europe is much more traumatic but also has its advantages. If you destroy domestic businesses which are no longer viable because of the lack of credit and domestic demand, and you send people to the dole queue, in the end those people can only find work in those production sectors which for the moment will be fundamentally be exporters, until domestic demand recovers. In other words, you reallocate resources to the production activities without public intervention to temper that radical change. This generates a greater fall in the economy, more unemployment, but possibly in the medium and long term a better reallocation of resources. In other words, it seems that when Spain emerges from the crisis it will have an economy which exports more and has more savings, less debt and less dependency on foreign investment, but it will still have too much unemployment!

This will be traumatic for many families because the adjustment will be slow. Hence the emergence of parties like Podemos, which channel this popular unease. A better option would have been greater flexibility from Germany to allow a less restrictive fiscal policy and a much more expansive and selective monetary policy. You only have to see how now, in delayed fashion, the ECB is trying to correct this, while we are seeing the beginnings of a bubble in public debt of countries like Germany itself (and perhaps in its real estate sector).

Having come this far with adjustment and seen families suffer so much, it makes no sense now to undo everything and cry over spilt milk. The Spanish economy will grow in the coming years and the growth will be more compensated and less dependent on external financing. Although when it begins to grow strongly we will soon see the entry of foreign capital investing in debt and once again we will see the same behaviours of domestic markets as in other cycles, starting with a rise in house prices which has occurred on previous occasions. In the USA house prices have now been recovering since the end of 2012.

In addition, however, fiscal discipline also has other advantages: initial public debt is less than in the model used by the USA. Let's not forget that Europe currently has a trade surplus (the USA has a deficit) and less debt as a percentage of its GDP than the USA. In other words, not everything is bad for Europe.

What I cannot agree with is that the anti-deficit crisis resolution model we have applied in Europe will improve its competitiveness. This is a recurring theme in the media but it is not true. An economy with 27% unemployment cannot be more competitive than an economy with 8% unemployment. It has too many underused resources to be competitive. It will be able to export more because companies now have cheaper labour, but the economy as a whole continues to bear too heavy a burden, which is a very high level of unemployment. This burden will translate into an economic cost via unemployment benefits or a social and political cost which will end up being economic, because of the appearance of parties which propose sharing the wealth with workers who are unemployed and all those who are most affected by the crisis. In other words, extreme left parties like Podemos. It is not possible to have such a high level of unemployment without this affecting all citizens sooner or later.

When these unemployed are re-employed in jobs in sectors which generate profit, then we will be able to talk about a competitive country. But that will take time. If those sectors are cyclical, such as the real estate sector, then the competitiveness will last as long as money is earned in the sector and then it will be lost. You shouldn't pull the wool over people's eyes and tell them they are living in a better country when in reality many of the citizens are out of work. And even less so when youth employment exceeds 50%, compared to many countries in northern Europe where this rate is below 10%. Is it because employment legislation is not sufficiently flexible? Obviously not, because, as everybody knows, in Spain the employment market has great duality and young people are those who suffer from insecurity and lack of rights. It is said that during the crisis approximately 700,000 Spanish people have left to find work in other countries, principally because of a lack of opportunities in Spain. Also, many foreigners who came to Spain in the first decade of the 21st century to look for a better future have returned to their native countries.

There are no magic mechanisms for reallocating the workforce; in the end a company hires a worker if the marginal income it receives for that worker exceeds the marginal cost of having him or her. In other words, if it earns money by contracting that worker. And this applies to the short, medium and perhaps long term. But nobody hires workers if they are not a source of profit in the long term.

Consequently, the best investment a country can make is in its citizens' qualifications. A country with highly qualified workers generates a greater added value in its production of goods and services; not only will its workers earn better salaries, but the employment will also be less sensitive to the cycle. An example of this is Germany. There, being a Doctor is considered prestigious and the tendency is to study as much as possible. In Spain it used to be High School Graduates, then university graduates, but there are still only few Doctors. The evolution is a positive one, because the starting point was worse. Quality education is fundamental in any country and Spain must invest particularly in such education. If you compare public spending figures on education with other countries, figures from 2012 put Spain in 90th position of 175 in proportion to its GDP. This is a low figure. If we compare what is spent on education compared to public spending as a whole, we would be in position 149 of 175. The fundamental cause is in the spending allocated to university education. Harvard and Stanford universities alone receive more income than the whole of the Spanish public university system. We have to redefine our public spending priorities.

It is surprising that Spain allocates less public spending on Education as a percentage of its GDP than the USA, a country which places a fundamental stake on a private teaching model.

I believe we have made great progress, and this also applies to education; in fact, despite the exaggerated cycle we have experienced because of our joining the Euro, a misguided monetary policy and a fiscal policy which was too passive, the economic history of Spain over the last 30 years has been a success. I don't share the thinking of those who use the crisis as an excuse to want to reform everything. Crises are moments when changes have to be made, but we shouldn't go crazy.

As I have said, Education in Spain has improved greatly, has become more generalised, and the creation of private universities and the mixed private-public model have allowed quality education at a reasonable price. Little by little this has had a positive effect on the economy and will continue to do so in the future. But it is also true that, looking at the comparisons, and taking into account the differences in income between people and regions, in Spain we should have more public spending on education.

Returning to the issue at hand, because we are part of the Euro today we have a high level of unemployment. As the devaluation of real salaries has been slow because the employment market is usually quite inflexible and adjusts very slowly, at the end of the crisis the level of unemployment is very high. This means that the economy as a whole has a problem of excessive social and economic cost. And although companies might be competitive at the beginning of the recovery, the economy as a whole is not, because it has to pay unemployment benefits and unemployed workers do not generate production. This, in turn, means that public deficit continues to be high and public debt continues to grow.

And this is not a trivial matter because at the end of the crisis the so-called peripheral countries of Europe find themselves with a high level of unemployment and an excessive public and private debt. In Spain, private debt, which was high, has been reduced by 40% compared to GDP during the crisis, whereas public debt has increased by 60%.

Although we now have growth, job creation will be slow and it will take many years before we return to the levels of employment we had before the crisis, with the problems this will create on a social level.

Let's imagine that the next recession is delayed because of the major crisis we have experienced and the great excess capacity that has been generated. Let's suppose that the next crisis is in 2019 or 2020 and that the recession will be neither very long nor very hard. Even in a case like this, it will not have given time to countries like Spain and Greece to reduce their debt or their unemployment sufficiently to be able to take countercyclical measures. Although we can implement fiscal stimuli such as the Plan E (which, I insist, worked in the short term even though almost certainly there was no investment in production for the long term), any of these fiscal stimuli, be that greater public spending or a reduction in taxes, in the short term will always generate greater public deficit. This, added to the public and private debt there may be at the time, could hasten the end of the Euro. This risk exists and is a very serious one. The countries in the Euro zone should start to study how this problem can be solved in the long term.

Certain measures which the affected countries could take spring to mind, but all of them are bad ones. They are bad because if you reduce public spending in the short term, this has a negative impact on the economy, and if there are already very high levels of unemployment, then the solution is a bad one. There won't be a major reduction in public spending during the economic recovery and even less so with the arrival of extreme left parties.

The conclusion is that Spain, Greece and Italy should not have entered the Euro. Once you are in, you have to focus on the overseas dependence of economies. Because capital in the Euro zone will always go to the safest country when there is a crisis, and in the next crisis the safest country will not be Greece, Spain or Italy. This means that Spain, over the next few years, must focus on what it is basically trying to do, which is not stimulate its domestic demand too much and focus on exporting more, and making its employment market more flexible to improve its competitive position. But the cost of this will be increasing social inequalities. If it doesn't do so in time, in the next crisis it will leave the Euro. There will be no way of keeping it in. Or, at least, this will be much more likely to be the case.

If the extreme left parties are elected to government and they decide to stimulate domestic demand excessively by increasing public deficit, Spain will leave the Euro in the next crisis. You can only apply these expansive policies if there is support from the other countries in the European Union and from the European Central Bank, which does not appear to be the case; you only have to look at the case of Greece, which is pitiful to say the least.

Greek and Spanish citizens should have received more information from their politicians about the risks involved in joining the Euro. Because once you are in, getting out is very traumatic and generates too many problems. In the case of Greece, the best thing they could do today is leave the Euro, because any future scenario involves the same problem: high indebtedness and an economy which cannot pay its debts. The best thing would be for them to leave the Euro and enter a devalued drachma which, to begin with, would bring high inflation and make it impossible to buy foreign products, but which would be the solution to make the debt smaller; by redenominating it in drachma it would be a kind of debt relief. This new devalued drachma with higher interest rates and its own Central Bank would attract foreign capital again. In addition, exports would rise thanks to being in the new currency, and imports would fall. The external balance would improve considerably. The Greeks would be poorer in as much as their assets would be worth less overseas, but their debt would also be smaller.

Spain is not in the same situation, because its debt is sustainable and its public deficit appears to be more or less under control. The growth it is experiencing from the lowest levels of the cycle seems to indicate a recovery. The social and political problem of high unemployment levels and high debt continues to exist. Only history will tell whether these are serious problems or problems which will be corrected little by little.

Fortunately for the countries of southern Europe, I believe that European recovery will be slow. There is considerable excess production capacity and I don't think the economy will increase with too much intensity in the European Union in the coming years. This will mean that production will continue below its potential for a considerable time and there will be no inflationary tensions; the economy will not overheat again and the countries of southern Europe will have very favourable financing conditions with low interest rates for a prolonged period of time.

Unemployment will be corrected gradually if nobody goes crazy with communist economic planning policies, and Spain will emerge from the crisis.

Here we return to the previous points: if we want to reduce unemployment, and if we want workers and business people to earn more, we have to improve the productivity of our production factors; this includes having better education (not only spending more, but more efficiently), having cheaper energy, whether that means fracking or any other type of energy investment which reduces the cost of the energy and dependence on overseas.

These are long-term solutions which we must start to adopt as a country, while being aware that it is not easy. There is a need for powerful public investment policies and stimuli for private investment. We need to liberalise the markets so that well-managed companies can survive crises better and improve the total productivity of the economy. We need to eliminate administrative obstacles and intervention or excessive regulation which does not favour the best but rather the one who has the best contacts.

This liberalisation must also occur in politics, and parties must focus more on the citizens and less on themselves. They have to open up their electoral lists. They have to increase their transparency and improve public services with greater competition between them.

The administration must introduce competitiveness criteria, such as the example of Madrid, where people can now choose their doctor. Public management and public services must introduce efficiency mechanisms and for this we need competition. But one thing we have learned from the crisis is that regulation is necessary. An investment bank cannot be a commercial bank, as occurred after the Crash of 1929. A bank should not be able to devote itself to housing development, which unfortunately is what some of them are doing right now with no legal limit.

Chapter 3: is Spain not competitive?

It is curious to hear economists, or journalists specialising in Economics, often say that Spain is not a competitive country, and defend their argument by saying that Spain has a trade balance with a deficit (it sells less overseas than it buys) and for that reason we are not competitive.

This is not the case. Whether a country has a positive or negative trade balance depends more on whether the rest of the world is prepared to lend it money or buy assets in that country than its ability to sell. It also depends on the saving patterns of the country's inhabitants. In other words, if the trade deficit is not financed because foreigners buy houses in Spain or because they lend us money then there is no way we can spend more than we earn and there is no way for a deficit to exist, regardless of whether that country's products are better or worse. If, on the other hand, we Spanish were bigger savers and didn't like to spend, there wouldn't be a deficit either because we would consume less than we sell.

The trade balance has more to do with the saving patterns of a country's citizens and of the perception lenders have of that country than with its overseas competitiveness. It is true that if an economy sells high quality manufactured products and buys non-manufactured products, then it is easier to save, but not necessarily. For example, China sells relatively non-manufactured products and yet it has a trade surplus because its citizens consume little. At the opposite end of the scale, Japan sells highly manufactured products, as does the USA, yet in recent times both of them have had trade deficits.

According to World Bank and OECD figures, exports in Spain represented 32% of the country's GDP in 2014, and in 2010 Spain exported 25.5% of its GDP. We can compare this, for example, with the USA, which in 2013 exported 13.5% of its GDP. In 2010 Greece exported 22% and in 2014 exported 33%.

It is clear that a number of factors influence exports, primarily the size of the economy. The USA is a very large country with an enormous domestic market, which means that this market has grown so much that its percentage of exports is lower. On the other hand, however, the financing it receives also has an influence, depending on the confidence international investors have in the solvency of its economy. Even today, the USA, despite the crisis, has a trade deficit and has not corrected its imbalances. Its exports have increased from 12.4% of its GDP in 2010 to 13.5% in 2014. Imports increased from 13.16% to 13.83%. US citizens continue to be able to consume products and services despite the crisis, and American companies did not have to sell them overseas. Domestic demand remained strong thanks to the fact that its government stimulated its economy by generating public deficit which in turn could be financed by the Fed, its own Central Bank. This is something which does not happen with the countries of southern Europe. Thanks to this financing by the Fed, the dollar was weakened for a few years, which helped to increase North American exports slightly.

In Greece, however, and in Spain to a lesser extent, when confidence in their economies falls, companies have to go and look for demand outside the country because the citizens of that country have fewer resources. They do not receive financing and the State cannot spend what it should. Citizens reduce their private debt (in Spain by 40% of GDP since the start of the crisis) and consume less within the country. Domestic companies' exports increase because they look for customers outside the country to a greater degree than its citizens' imports increase. The economy grows because of exports, because domestic demand does not receive the overseas capital through financing or the purchase of assets. Confidence in Spain and Greece falls and the situation can only be remedied by selling more overseas.

Exports during the crisis have grown more in Greece than in Spain. Why is this the case if it is supposed that they have taken fewer measures than the Spanish? The Greek economy is more dependent on overseas than the Spanish economy; it is an island with fewer inhabitants and a much smaller domestic market. When financing dries up in the private sector, the Greeks begin to export more, from 22% of GDP in 2010 to 33% in 2014, whereas in Spain the rise is from 25.5% to 32%. In other words, exports increase proportionally more in Greece, as a result of the crisis and the fall in private sector domestic demand.

Why, then, does Spain have a better external deficit? Because of its public sector. In Greece, the private sector adjusts and exports even more than the Spanish; Greek public spending continues to grow and now stands at 60% of GDP. This public sector continues to generate domestic demand. In fact, imports into Greece rose from 30.7% of GDP in 2010 to 35.3% of GDP in 2014. In Spain, however, public spending was reduced in those years as a percentage of GDP, and reached the figure of close to 43% of GDP (in 2012 it was 47% of GDP). The State is shrinking so that it can meet its public deficit objective. Hence imports rose in Spain from 26.8% of GDP in 2010 to 29.6% of GDP in 2014. In other words, in Spain imports increased by 2.8 percentage points in relation to its GDP in the period, whereas in Greece they increased by 4.6. In Greece the State continues to consume resources that it shouldn't consume. While the Greek private sector is starting to export, as in Spain, fundamentally because it has no alternative, its political class does not want to adjust public spending and consequently domestic demand increases. Furthermore, the worst of domestic demands is the one which is least efficient in the long term, that of the people around power. I am talking about those companies which do not have to look overseas to export but which live off the general budgets of the Greek state. Public spending in Greece would be fine, like the fiscal stimulus in the USA, if it had its own currency which could be devalued gradually as its Central Bank lowered interest rates and bought Greek debt. But this is not what happens in Europe. Here, Greece is getting into debt in a currency which does not belong to it and which is adapted to the reality of Europe as a whole and not just Greece.

The analysis is not so simple, but this is almost certainly a good explanation of the phenomenon. Perhaps I should also mention Spanish employment reform and its impact on domestic demand. This may also have a very positive effect on finances, even though citizens may not perceive it as such because they can consume and invest less in the short term; in the long term, however, they will be grateful for the measures which have been taken to make the country sustainable, bearing in mind that Spain is already in the Euro and that the countries of northern Europe are not prepared to share debt by creating Eurobonds to finance more public spending.

To a certain degree this is logical because it is a model, created by Ludwig Erhard, which worked very well for the Germans. The liberalisation of markets and the creation of an economy which lives fundamentally from exports. The problem is when an attempt is made for the whole of Europe to live from exports. This is very difficult, because the currency will tend to gain in value and not all the countries will be competitive.

During this crisis, if Germany had had its own currency, the Deutschmark, money would have sought refuge there, as happened with the Swiss franc, and its exports would have fallen considerably. Germany would not be in its current situation and neither would the countries of southern Europe, because the peseta, the lira and the drachma would have depreciated, increasing exports from southern Europe, their economies would have grown more in relative terms and they would have had lower levels of unemployment. In other words, entering the Euro for these countries was a mistake.

It is foreseeable that in the short and medium term Spanish trade deficits will reduce and there may even be surpluses; in fact the country has been reducing its overseas financing for a number of years. This will not be the result of just greater competitiveness of our products but also, and fundamentally, the fact that foreigners are not so prepared to lend to us, to finance our trade deficits, and therefore Spanish companies have no alternative but to sell more overseas, where there is more demand.

When confidence in the Spanish economy returns, we may have trade deficits again, as is happening today in the United States.

The positive aspect of the rebalancing of the Spanish economy can be seen in the increase in exports which is, in part, a consequence of the necessary adjustment in real salaries and, on the other hand, because companies are looking overseas to sell their products and services. Is Spain more competitive now than it was before the crisis? Perhaps, although it is true to say that a country which had 26.4% unemployment in 2013, which is a considerable excess in production capacity, would not appear to be a competitive country. It may be that functioning companies which have workers with lower salaries because of the excess supply in the employment market are competitive, but the country itself has lost competitiveness. A company with excess capacity may sell more because it reduces its prices to occupy capacity and achieve a lower unit cost of production, but it will not be more competitive than a company operating at its optimum level of capacity. If exports grow, it is not because of the economy's increased competitiveness as a whole but because companies have no domestic demand and look overseas. We only have to look at the way exports have evolved in Greece. It is the companies which are increasing their competitiveness because they have more attractive prices resulting from lower costs derived from the excess capacity of that economy. But an economy with 26.4% unemployment is not more competitive than when it had 8% unemployment. Just as the fact that Spain, which exports 32% of its GDP, is not more competitive than the USA which exports 13.5% of its GDP. It exports more because it has to go overseas to sell.

This is why Germany and Japan became exporting countries. They lost the Second World War, their countries were left devastated, with economies which were very dependent on overseas capital and very low levels of domestic demand. This meant that they made use of the industrial resources left over from the war, starting with the workforce, and focused on exporting.

This is why today an economy as powerful as that of Germany exported 45.6% of its GDP in 2014. Although it is also true to say that this figure is as high as it is thanks to the Euro and the advantages it offers Germany.

If we look at Japan, where exports represent 16.2% of its GDP, we see that this is because the yen appreciated for a long period because Japan was a refuge market in Asia. For a long time the Japanese Central Bank erroneously allowed deflation with an insufficient monetary base. Now, fortunately, they are trying to devalue the yen and create inflation. Germany would be in a very similar position to Japan if it was not in the Euro.

However, Luxembourg has a level of exports representing 203.3% of its GDP, the United Arab Emirates has 99.5%, Hong Kong 219.6% and Switzerland 72.1% of its GDP in 2013. This explains how exports also depend on the size of the economies (the smaller it is the more it tends to export because it cannot sell at home) and of the flows of capital they receive through fiscal incentives or other reasons.

To sum up, Germany has financed itself with money from the peripheral countries and has had a currency which is much more devalued than the Deutschmark would have been. If Germany had been outside the Euro, it would have levels of exports as a percentage of its GDP which are much lower than those it currently has, and during the crisis its exports would have suffered more. This is not a question of competitiveness, it is a question of exchange rate and size of the country (of its domestic economy), and of the confidence foreign investors have to invest in that country or keep their money in that country. It would be desirable, given that it has benefited from the Euro, for Germany to contribute more to solving the problems of unemployment in southern Europe. This is something we must demand of them. Yes, they are the creditors, but they are also the beneficiaries of Monetary Union in the terms in which it was created. And we only have to look at the figures as proof: a high level of unemployment in southern Europe and high exports in Germany, with low unemployment and no fiscal deficit.

Exports are also affected by other factors, such as geographical location. This is why Spain cannot be Denmark or Belgium. Spain is a country which has greater growth potential than other rich countries where the costs are greater and where the potential for improving the training of its workers is less; this will mean that, when growth returns, financing will come into play again and almost certainly the trade deficit will continue to exist in the long term. This is much more likely if the parties which promote an increase in public spending and, consequently, domestic demand are in government. The situation of reducing trade deficit or the appearance of surplus will surely be a fleeting phenomenon. For a German, it is much more attractive to invest in his own currency in a country where costs are lower and there is greater potential for training the workforce, and consequently for improving the production factors, than in a country where the workers earn more and the workforce is already qualified.

If you are still not convinced by these explanations, you only have to think of the United States. Do you think that a country like the USA, which has some of the best universities in the world and the best technological companies, is not a competitive country? Obviously not. Its trade deficit exists because foreign citizens want to buy US assets because they appear more solvent or safer, and more attractive. This applies to buying assets or buying debt. They are two sides of the same coin which finance American consumers, who continue to use foreign resources buying more than they produce. But this does not mean that the USA is not a competitive country.

Does everything depend on external financing? No. You can have a culture of saving which means that little is consumed and, nonetheless, work or invest a lot (which is what occurs in developing countries like China). This is certainly a factor which also explains what is happening in Germany, but it also explains what is happening in tax havens like Luxembourg, Hong Kong and Switzerland. There is a lot of saving because capital comes in from overseas and that capital allows the creation of exporting companies which also look for tax breaks. It is incoming capital, but because it is to invest fundamentally in shares or company debt, the citizens of those countries do not spend it. Let's think, for example, of the pharmaceutical companies Roche and Novartis, or the company Nestlé. Or of companies which have moved their European headquarters to Switzerland, like Procter & Gamble for example.

Also, if the citizens of a country save a lot, like the Chinese, and invest a lot, in the end they manage to export more than they import and thus generate trade surpluses. This is the opposite of what happens in Brazil.

Ireland, which has a tax system which is very advantageous for companies, exported 105.3% of its GDP in 2014. It imported 84.5% of the GDP. It is home to the headquarters, for example, of Google in Europe.

Singapore, as we have already said, exported 187% and imports 163.2%. Macao exports 99.1% and imports 44.7%. The

UAE exports 99%, as we have said, and imports 86.1%. Switzerland exports 72.1% and imports 60%. Luxembourg exports 203% and imports 168.1%. In other words, the conclusion is that if a country, like Spain, does not want to be dependent on overseas financing and have a healthy economy which has no problems in future crises, what it must do is create a favourable tax system for companies. This favourable tax system will lead to more exporting companies setting up in the country, and more growth in existing companies. In the end this will have the effect of increasing its trade balance and its fiscal income. It is much easier to tax exports of products than what is sold in a bar or restaurant.

But it is not always the case that there has to be low public spending as a proportion of GDP for a country to export a lot. Denmark exports 53.7% of its GDP and imports 48.4%. Its public spending as a proportion of GDP is close to 58%.

It appears, then, that the geographical location, international agreements (like being in the European Union), the size of the country, overseas confidence, the behaviour of domestic consumers and taxation are the fundamental determining factors in a country's trade balance. But you also have to add a country's currency to this. Denmark, for example, has maintained the Danish crown as a mechanism for domestic devaluations which allow it to export more in times of crisis, although its fluctuation is closely associated with the evolution of the Euro. In other words, they are keeping the cartridge in the chamber just in case.

Google, Apple, Dell, Procter & Gamble, Caterpillar and a long list of companies make it patently obvious that the American problem is not one of competitiveness. The same is true with Spain, although on a different scale. This is why, when the gurus of economic programming tell us that we have to change our production model, have more industry, or more whatever, they have to let entrepreneurs invest in what makes them money and stop programming economic activity in industries which surely would not be competitive. They have to let those who invest in the wrong place go to the wall, and those who invest in the right place earn money. The State must only intervene to moderate cycles, when there are possible bubbles or to stimulate sectors (for example, cinema or art) or desirable behaviour (investment in research and development or in training its citizens).

But as far as the economy in general is concerned, it will be the market itself and the business people and investors themselves who will look for what is most profitable for them and not what is dictated by an academic planning the future of the country. History demonstrates that five-year plans work badly. This was explained very well in the past by theorists from the Austrian School of Economics, in particular Ludwig von Mises and Friedrich Hayek.

Spain needs to invest in improving the training of its citizens, and needs to create the incentives which make these students pursue their search for excellence and ensure ongoing improvement; and it needs to create the necessary seed for the start-up of new business initiatives which are innovative and have high added value.

Charles Cobb and Paul Douglas, professors at the University of Chicago, described an equation drawn from a regression analysis theoretically proposed by Knut Wicksell, which we will talk about later, which explains the production in an economy in terms of work, capital and a coefficient called "total factors productivity". Communist or economic programming economists, who are now talking about new production models, tried to invest in those sectors and those production factors where they believed that production would increase the most. Time demonstrated that in the long term, a capitalist economy distributes the production factors better to generate greater production than where the academics decide to invest.

The USSR carried out experiments to liberalise agricultural markets which demonstrated that growth was much greater when the resources were distributed by the private economy than when it was done by the State. This is fundamentally because workers have a greater incentive to work thanks to the rewards they receive in a capitalist economy. The same thing happened in China, and the Guanzhoug free trade area established in 1984 has demonstrated this; Chinese politicians have realised this and have taken steps to liberalise their economy.

In Spain, however, we are still talking about a new production model. The State can establish incentives to stimulate sectors or improve free competition conditions by liberalising markets (particularly those which come from monopolies), but no matter how much it wants to, it cannot change the production model. When it does so, the story usually ends up badly.

Chapter 4: is Spain a country which produces little?

Another frequent error is to consider Spanish people non-productive and the Spanish economy as producing little. Our economy has a very high component in the services sector and the construction sector.

In Spain, financial services and tourist services, together with the real estate sector and the public works construction sector have been the great motors of the economy in recent years. These sectors are traditionally labour intensive and produce little. When you are involved in tourism, and you have a hotel or restaurant, you frequently need to occupy the rooms and the tables. To maintain the hotel you need cleaning staff, people on reception, and so on, and a restaurant needs waiters. The product generated or the earnings generated for each room or each table by a restaurant or hotel staff is much lower than that generated by an operator in a functioning factory producing a top of the range car or producing an advanced technology chip.

In essence, in the sectors where the Spanish economy is more at the cutting edge, there is low productivity per worker, because the activity they carry out has no room for large increases in productivity.

If, for example, you build a factory which produces a top of the range car, the product generated by the factory has a very high sale value in the market. When you reach a certain point in volume of sales, the total product per worker is very high. The productivity of the workers in the factory is very high. Economies of scale occur, the cost of production per unit goes down substantially and, consequently, the productivity per worker for that product, once it is sold in the market, improves substantially. The same is not true with a hotel or with a real estate development. The hotel's capacity is very limited by its size: we are not talking about a product where you can produce large economies of scale by amortising fixed costs. The hotel's maximum is 100 rooms, and even when it is full you cannot occupy 150, you cannot produce more. You can increase the price of the room to reach an optimum level, but you will always earn less than if you can produce 100 more cars with very little increase in prices. If you increase the price of the room from 100 to 150, your earnings will increase by 50%, in other words 5,000 more. If you can produce 100 more cars at the same price, you will earn 10,000 more. It is easier to increase production in a factory than rooms in a hotel.

The same thing happens with real estate developments. You can build 100 houses, and that is the limit; town planning limits do not allow you to build 1000 and thereby generate more economies of scale. In addition, if you want to build more you need more personnel. In other words, the productivity of each worker is limited. As there is considerable limitation in the reclassification of land, the tendency is for prices to go up more than production, and as production has a very intensive labour cost, almost everything is a variable cost and generates few economies of scale.

What's more, in a high technology factory, like the factories in Germany or Japan, where the quality of the engineering has achieved high quality products and where there is a competitive difference with other producers, productivity can be increased substantially if you sell more, until you reach the factory's capacity. As we have said, the maximum capacity of the factory is greater than that of a hotel or restaurant for example, which are much more limited by space.

This means that a worker's productivity is lower in Spain than it might be in Germany or Japan. In turn, this means that when there is a change of economic cycle the marginal productivity of the work (what is produced additionally by each added unit in the work factor) falls more in Spain than in Germany or Japan, with the consequent greater destruction of employment in Spain. This is also because Spain's employment market is less flexible, and until recently salaries could not go down, and even went up, even though workers were being fired at the same time.

This phenomenon can also be seen in the United States. If you look at unemployment in California, where the real estate sector is bigger than in Massachusetts, you will see that the unemployment figures are higher in California because its economy is more linked to the cycle and, in addition, the average productivity of Californian workers is less than their counterparts in Massachusetts. In both cases, however, the unemployment levels are much lower than those in Europe.

For this reason, even if Spanish governments insist on making the employment market more flexible, Spain will continue to have more unemployment than Germany in future crises. Unless the flexibility is so high that much less is paid per worker than it is now. Social security contributions are excessively high compared to the countries around us. For lower salaries we have higher contributions, almost certainly because we have a very good social security system with a very good public health system.

The more flexible the market is, the less unemployment will grow in the next crisis, but there will also be a greater difference in income between citizens. If we do not want a repeat in the next cycle of the high unemployment we had in 1995 and in 2012, not only does there have to be a low firing cost but fundamentally there has to be a low hiring cost (which includes the firing cost) or high productivity. High productivity is achieved by generating businesses with added value where there is a sustainable competitive advantage and where the activity itself is very productive. In other words, Spain must be not only a country where there is a high component in the services sector (bars, restaurants and hotels) but also one with a high level of industrial production of good quality and services with a great added value.

To achieve this, the Spanish government must focus fundamentally on the long term and on supply policies. In other words, it must improve education, by making it more competitive and accessible. If Spain wants to have an economy with a low level of employment, it must have high quality engineers who are prepared to remain in Spain and who can obtain financing for their new projects.

Priority must be given to qualified training, making it more democratic and more accessible, not only for those with the best CVs. There must be investment in professional qualifications. For a long time, being an engineer in Spain was a privilege reserved for those with the best academic results, which was a select and reduced group. The liberalisation of university teaching, initiated by the governments of Felipe Gonzalez, has increased the number of engineers and this will be noted in the long term in the country's economy.

But it is not just a question of having a lot of engineers; education must also be competitive. For this to happen, a country must attract engineers from overseas, and this is only achieved with better pay. This is a consequence of the liberalisation of the profession and of the existence of real competition to gain access to professor positions in universities. For this to happen, a university student must pay a large part of the cost of his or her training and not receive low quality training because he or she doesn't want to pay for it. Or the State must invest in that education by introducing competition mechanisms between teachers and professors, with appropriate remuneration. If a mixed system is introduced, this influences the level of the education. We will talk about this in a later chapter.

The fact that someone studies at a university in the United States and there is a large number of foreign students and professors explains that in its education system there is free competition and the best people gain access to the best positions, which are well paid, and the students want to go to their classes because they know they will receive the best teaching. This is what happens with football in Spain. The world's best footballers play here because they are paid appropriately for it. There is free competition.

This model also exists in Spain in business schools, the Instituto de Empresa (IE), IESE or ESADE attract talent from overseas, teachers and students who come from other countries because the education is competitive. However, the same is not true of training in other fields. I am not saying that an engineer from ICAI or from the Polytechnic University (UP) is bad; what I am saying is that knowledge must be opened up to free competition and must also reach more people. It is obvious that these universities have great prestige despite the fact that their financial resources are limited.

Having said all this, we also have to explain that the statistics do not reflect what we, the EGB[11] generation, have seen.

---

[11] Educación General Básica: system of secondary education which was replaced in Spain in 1996/97

102

On average, the people who have joined the employment market in recent decades are more qualified than ever. Spain has improved a great deal in the last twenty years: its economy, its infrastructures, its health system, education, its social security, and so on. Spain is a success story in democracy. Anyone who has lived in the 1980s and 1990s and the 21st century knows this. Workers today are much more qualified than they were at the beginning of democracy. The country works much better despite the crisis we have had and we cannot throw overboard all the great work which has been carried out in these years just because in recent years we have had a major economic crisis which was a result of previous excesses and worsened by our entry into the Euro.

The best way of showing that this has been the case is to compare the evolution of income per capita in Spain with that of the United States since the start of the 20th century. This process of convergence is very well explained in Juan Velarde's book called '100 Years of Spanish Economy'[12].

---

[12] Juan Velarde: "Cien años de Economía española". Ediciones encuentro S.A. 2009.

Chapter 5: other considerations on the Spanish economy

THE ACCUMULATION OF CAPITAL

Much is said about the lack of entrepreneurship in Spain, which is attributed to a conservative character, fear of failure, etc. I prefer to think that low levels of entrepreneurship have been linked to two factors, primarily low qualifications. This problem has been corrected over time. Secondly, and for me the most important factor, is low capitalisation of the population.

There are rich aristocrats in Spain, there are rich people linked to regulated sectors, and there are rich politicians, but there aren't too many rich people in non-regulated sectors because the markets are subject to more intervention than in countries like the

USA or Germany. This has been corrected gradually because Spain has grown considerably in the last 30 years, but there is insufficient wealth amongst private individuals to generate a lot of entrepreneurship.

Why do I say this? If a person is a multimillionaire, he won't mind investing and losing a million Euros or so on a project by a young promising entrepreneur. This is the case of Ross Perot in NeXT, a Steve Jobs project in which he invested $20 million.

But if all the money is in the hands of the State, or those extractive elites, and there are no incentives to take risks, nobody will be a business angel. As a general rule, the State gives fewer productive subsidies in the medium and long term than the investments that private investors can make. Clearly there are other incentives. I am not saying this is always true: one example of highly profitable public financing was the R+D+I of the discovery of America. There, the "State" got it right and discovered America, and the gold obtained subsequently made it a profitable business. But in the end, the English model of Private R+D+ I triumphed. Over time, it proved to be a better option than the assignment of resources carried out by the Catholic Monarchs. In the long term, planned economies fail and free ones triumph. The incentives are different, and history repeats itself over and over again.

It is clear that when we emerge from this crisis we have to consider which services we want the State to provide us with. We have to decide whether we need a municipal sports centre in every town, a cultural centre with English classes, whether it is necessary to have a music Conservatory in every town or a public municipal theatre, or a real estate company which builds free housing instead of protected housing. All these services have to be paid for, and because they are normally underused they usually cost a lot and generate little income. But they have a harmful effect on the private economy because not only do they reallocate resources inefficiently, but they also occupy the place of a business set up by a Physical Education student or an English teacher who wants to set up a private language school or a music teacher who wants to give private classes. They distort the real price of the market. Although if you ask a music teacher whether he or she wants to see classes in the Conservatory, they will say yes; what they don't know is that they will earn less when they set up their own school because people can go to the Conservatory and pay less than if it were a private school.

The same thing happens with doctors in Spain, who complain that they earn little. They earn little because there is a big public health system. If such a system did not exist, the customer would pay the necessary price for the service and almost certainly they would earn more. The State plays the role of middleman influencing his or her salary, and in exchange provides security.

I am not saying here that the State should not provide public health; in this aspect I do believe that both Health and Education, where the latter is understood to be what is studied at School, in the Sixth Form and at University, should continue with the current system, which is a mixed public-private system. We should, however, be aware that it is a system which costs a lot and needs to be rationalised and have its deviations corrected.

If I am going to have an expensive system, I want it to be in Health and in Education, but not to provide non-essential services which every individual can choose to consume in the private market, allowing entrepreneurs and workers to earn money according to their qualifications.

In my opinion, a very large proportion of spending, as is the case now, should go on Health and Education, and also on Security and Defence.

The fact that there are few rich people in Spain is not only because the State interferes in the business of private individuals, but also because taxes are excessively high because the number of public administrations is excessive. The fact that you are placing a stake on a fiscal stimulus solution for this crisis does not mean that you do not want to reduce unnecessary spending.

In Spain there are 17 autonomous parliaments, plus two more for Ceuta and Melilla. It is calculated that there may be more than 70,000 politicians, including mayors and councillors, autonomous MPs, members of provincial parliaments, national MPs and senators, heads of island councils and councillors for the Valle de Arán.

The fact that everyone in the State of Autonomous governments wants a slice of the cake has led to the more historic bodies wanting more powers and, on the other hand, to the rest wanting more powers, thus creating new management structures which have multiplied spending. What is paradoxical about this system is that the autonomous governments have been created, with their consequent cost, but Central Government has not seen a reduction in spending to reflect the powers it has lost.

I am a firm believer in the State of Autonomous Governments: their existence has improved public services and has increased the responsibility of the regional administration with regard to voters. In addition, as Milton Friedman explained, this competition between regions, as with competition between towns, is very positive for citizens, who benefit and gain more freedom. Now the politicians have to correct the excesses of a system created in fits and starts, which has grown to offer a good service, but in which no account has been taken of the cost because citizens were not aware of what it cost to maintain it, because it was being financed with more public debt and not taxes.

GROWTH VERSUS FAIRNESS

The countries which have seen the most economic growth in the 20th century are the Anglo-Saxon countries, plus others like Germany and Japan, influenced by the USA after defeat in the Second World War. This is fundamentally because of the economic freedom in their economies. Economic freedom produces the correct incentives for economies to develop. The prize for a job well done is to earn money. In socialist or planned economies we do not find the correct incentives, and the priority is not to sell to the customer but to make contact with the civil servant, and pull strings. This is an incorrect incentive which does not generate wealth, only corruption.

If you compare the United States or South Korea with communist countries like Cuba, North Korea or Vietnam, you can clearly see the difference between the two models. The best way to see success in terms of growth of the capitalist economy is to observe how China has grown in recent years as it has progressively liberalised its economy. Back in the former Soviet

Union, trials were carried out with farmers who were given ownership of the land, and the yields were much greater.

What emerges clearly from this is that the best thing for a country's growth is a capitalist economy. However, in an economy it is also necessary to have a level of fairness so that everyone comes out winning. Anyone who has travelled to the United States will have been surprised by the social differences there are compared to Europe. This translates not only into a problem of social fairness but also a problem of lack of security. You see more police officers and security as being more necessary to keep the social peace.

Can you imagine the USA with 27% unemployment like Spain? It is often said that it is the family in Spain which supports the unemployed and allows these levels of unemployment to exist without social conflict; I believe the reality is more complex than this and also includes a system of greater social protection which is not as badly managed as people think. This is possibly why the phenomenon of the extreme left parties has only occurred at the end of the crisis and after employment reform was approved, with the elimination of the civil servants' extra pay packet and the increase in VAT and property tax, which have hit the poorest classes hardest.

Raising VAT and property tax indiscriminately does not make much sense when they are taxes which, by their very nature, have a greater effect on those with lower earnings. It would have been more reasonable to raise income tax on the highest incomes or raise the wealth tax to a certain degree. It is true that in the end everything was raised, but VAT and property tax should have been the last options.

Whatever the case, in Spain we complain a lot that we pay high taxes and receive few services, that money has been wasted on many useless projects; while true, this may only be true in part. We have accomplished many things in these years of democracy: the country has been modernised and wealth has been created, and although the crisis has been too hard-hitting to be overlooked, what took place prior to it was a long period of well-being which greatly improved everyone's quality of life. As José Carlos Díez explains very well in his book "There is life after the crisis"[13], this model of greater public spending and higher taxes provides a better quality of life and greater security than that which exists in many Latin American countries where there are major social differences and the state is much smaller. Furthermore, in my opinion, this social stability has contributed to the growth of economies throughout the

---

[13] José Carlos Díez. "Hay vida después de la Crisis". Plaza y Janes. Ed. Radom House Mondadori, S.A. May, 2013

20th century after the great collective failure caused by the two World Wars. In other words, there is a point where economic freedom is very good for generating wealth but when it generates too much social instability it destroys it. And there is a point where the Welfare State can be very positive for generating wealth. The key is in generating a fair balance between growth promoted by free competition and "social justice" or fairness.

The fledgling recovery is the right time to correct the imbalances generated by a crisis of these characteristics between the most disadvantaged citizens and those who, either because of their training, their prudence or their wealth (either saved or inherited) have managed to emerge from it better.

It is the time to promote social policies which allow unemployment to be reduced in the short term, both with fiscal stimulus policies and policies to liberalise sectors. I do not think now is the time to reduce income tax; it would be better to reduce other taxes such as social security contributions or VAT. But we should be careful not to go too far, because this is not a case of generating once again an explosive domestic demand which feeds another period of private individuals taking on too much debt. Now, in 2015, we are at a point where consumer confidence is starting to recover and it may be more interesting to lower taxes than increase spending. I appear to be contradicting myself here, but that is not the case: at the moment of panic during the crisis the best measure is to increase public spending because it directly increases domestic demand, and when the situation begins to calm down, lowering taxes may be a better option because it is fairer, or it is easier to make it fairer. Whatever the case, with the current levels of unemployment, any measure which promotes employment is a positive one.

Now public sector debt has increased too much and needs to be corrected. When taxes are reduced, the best thing would be to reduce them moderately so as not to generate in the economic cycle more volatility than it usually has. In this sense I agree with Keynes in that we have to take advantage of growth to reduce the deficit and, if possible, generate a surplus which allows us to intervene in the economy in crisis with a fiscal stimulus.

Given that being in the Euro prevents us from financing these stimuli as we would wish, I believe the best thing we could do is to consider a serious savings plan as a country which allows us to stimulate the economy during the bad cycles (a kind of countercyclical reserve) which, although it might not save us from the next crisis, will reduce the effects. Collective savings plans have been used in other countries, such as Singapore, for example. It is not a new concept. It would be creating something like the countercyclical reserves which exist in the banking sector.

TRAINING, TRAINING AND TRAINING

In my personal spending I devote more than 50% of my earnings to the education of my children. This might seem crazy but I do not see it that way. My experience is that a good education, well used, generates more than acceptable returns on the investment, not just in economic terms but also in terms of enjoyment of life and personal prestige.

I am not saying that in Spain we should spend 50% of our budget on education, because logically health, unemployment insurance, pensions, the army, and domestic security are important; but I would double current spending to put us at higher levels than other countries. Public spending in Denmark on education was 8.55% of GDP in 2012, and in Spain it was 4.55%, like in Germany (4.81%). Almost certainly, in Germany private education is more important than in Spain. Because of the social differences and the fact that Spain is still a country with great differences between regions, there should be greater public spending on education, even higher than the spending in Denmark. Logically, with the controls and the quality they have in Denmark. Because very often it is not how much it costs but whether it is invested efficiently.

In this sense, the mixed system where there is private or approved quality education is also important. In the end, the fundamental advantage of private education is that it encourages competition and, consequently, improvement. Private schools which do not work tend to disappear more quickly than public schools which always receive the resources. It is important for there to be private schools and universities and also that there are public grants to allow students to study in these universities. The best students, irrespective of their income, should be able to go to the most prestigious universities, be they public or private.

As far as the public institutions are concerned, they should be given the necessary economic resources to enable them to attract talent which will ensure that the education is quality education. You can't have a good education if you don't pay teachers good salaries.

It is also necessary for public institutions to have measures to encourage excellence and competition. We are not saying that quality education should not be given to the less advantaged pupils, quite the opposite. What we are saying is that the best pupils should be allowed to go to the best quality public and private institutions. In Spain we have examples of public and private institutions of great quality. Moreover, public universities still enjoy great prestige within the country today.

On the same point, it is also necessary to rationalise the number of public universities throughout Spain, as they have increased in number more than necessary, with the consequent cost for State budgets and the resulting loss of quality for the system as a whole.

RESEARCH AND DEVELOPMENT

As with education, research and development are fundamental for the growth of the economy and the well-being of its citizens. Spending on research and development in Spain was 1.3% of GDP in 2012, compared to 2.92% in Germany and 2.79% in the United States.

Here the mixed public-private model is once again necessary in Spain. It is clear that R+D will certainly be much more efficient in the private sector than in the public sector, and for this reason there must be mechanisms which encourage investment in research and development. But if we take into account that a considerable part of Spanish technical universities are public, it is clear that public spending on research and development must also be considerable.

What we need are mechanisms of public-private co-operation which promote productive investment and do not spend money on projects which have no use. But it is also true that slack capacity, as the Anglo-Saxons call it, is also necessary. We need an excess of capacity so that there are creative projects. I believe that public investment in innovation and development channelled through the best quality public universities is fundamental. That way, we promote private projects which generate returns from this research and development.

As happened with the drive for industrialization at the beginning of the 20th century, during the Primo de Rivera dictatorship, today we also need to promote research which must be encouraged by both private initiative and public initiative.

LET'S RESTRUCTURE SPAIN

In his book "Postwar"[14], Tony Judt explains how the social democracies of southern Europe have been more concerned with creating major public structures than providing their citizens with services and appropriate social spending.

He contrasts Scandinavian social democracy with that of southern Europe and explains how in northern Europe the private economy generates sufficient earnings to defray the cost of major

---

[14] Tony Judt. "Postwar. A history of Europe since 1945". Ed. Taurus. Santillana Ediciones Generale, S.L. 2008

social spending, whereas in the countries of southern Europe there are not so many social resources because part of that spending has gone on creating a large public sector.

A few months ago I saw a chapter of the series "Free to Choose" which Milton Friedman did for American television, in which he explains that a large part of social spending for North American families went on the intermediary, i.e. on the State structure. This is the case with Spain: if we take social spending in Spain and divide it between the number of habitants with fewer resources, let's say the 25% of the population with the lowest earnings, we would get a very high figure per person.

Spain needs a restructuring of the country with a major reduction in its Public Administration. Let's suppose that the approximate figure of more than 70,000 public positions that exist in Spain each generate average spending on salary, travel, official cars, etc. of approximately €100,000 a year, which is quite conservative; in this case we would be talking about spending of €7 billion a year solely on public positions. This is more than the public universities receive in a year.

It is clear that there are too many autonomous parliaments, town councils, provincial councils and so on. The amount by which they should be reduced should be negotiated between the different political parties. A good criterion would be to keep sufficient

Administration to ensure good management of the resources and for there to be sufficient competition between the administrations.

If we then devoted these freed up resources to fundamentally improving the education of future generations, we would be doing great business.

The level of social spending in Spain has been shown to be very positive in a crisis as major as the one we have experienced. In his book "Fault Lines: How Hidden Fractures Still Threaten the World Economy", which I spoke about earlier, Raghuram Rajan said that the problem the USA had was that, because it had a very low level of social protection, its system was not designed to survive major crises. In a prolonged crisis over time, its system needed a great fiscal and monetary stimulus because it could not sustain high levels of unemployment because it had no social protection. However, he also said that it is a very good system for brief crises because, having a low level of protection, people who lose their jobs have a greater incentive to find a new one quickly in production sectors which have survived the crisis; creative destruction is given a boost and makes the Economy more competitive.

As a contrast to this system, he talked about the European system, where social protection is excessive and harmful for creative destruction during brief crises, as there are incentives not to look for work and remain on the dole queue, or for companies not to fire people so much because of the cost of doing so. Nevertheless, the European system was better for prolonged crises because it allowed for a higher level of unemployment without a major social crisis. This meant that the monetary and fiscal policy did not have to be so expansive, and thus emerging from the crisis would not be stimulating domestic demand and generating a trade deficit. Just the opposite of what happens in the United States.

And this is what is happening: the way in which Europe has solved its crisis is too traumatic for the unemployed in countries like Greece, Italy or Spain, but Europe will emerge from the crisis with a much more solid and secure economy than in the past. It will not be so dependent on overseas investment, as will have happened to the USA.

But is this social spending sustainable? It is obvious that for exceptional crises you have to take exceptional measures. It would have been desirable to have a special plan to help mortgage defaulters, which we did not have; we cannot say objectively that those who have not been able to pay their mortgage at the end of the crisis were those who got it wrong and, consequently, must pay for the consequences. Instead we can say that this crisis has been of such dimensions, almost certainly because the boom prior to it was so large and prolonged over time, that exceptional measures should have been taken.

Having said this, we also need to consider that this level of protection that we enjoy in Europe is not a be all and end all, and we have to see how the system can be adjusted so that it does not encourage unemployment and not working. The answer, as Aristotle would say, is to find a happy medium.

CRONY CAPITALISM?

In his book "Spain's Dilemma", Luis Garicano talks about crony Capitalism and describes it as one of the great scourges of the Spanish economy. He almost certainly has a better knowledge of these topics than I do. But it is also true to say that if we look at our daily life we can see a large number of companies: bars, restaurants, newsstands, clothes shops, food shops, services, etc. The great majority are companies which compete in a free market. To say that in Spain there is crony capitalism is, in my opinion, a great exaggeration.

It is evident that a large proportion of Spain's big companies come from regulated sectors or sectors which previously belonged to the public sector, but what has happened in Spain since the transition is precisely the opposite of crony capitalism.

Companies have grown in sectors which were not so regulated: Inditex, Mango, Mercadona and Grifols are in sectors where we cannot talk about crony capitalism. And there are thousands of small companies just like these big ones.

To talk of crony capitalism is to confuse a part with the whole. This is not what is happening in Spain. The fact that there has been cronyism and corruption in many sectors, especially those linked to the public sector and regulation, cannot lead us to think that Spain is a country where only the politicians or those around them earn money. This is false.

All we have to do is think of a friend or acquaintance who works in a Spanish or foreign company in a good position to realise that merit and skill also operate here. Perhaps it is not the same as in the USA, and almost certainly we cannot talk about the same level of economic freedom, but we are in a capitalist economy where good work receives its reward. Let's not forget, for example, that in the United States members of a same family are frequently Presidents of the country, which does not appear to be a very meritocratic system. But the system of elections is definitely democratic and appears to give equal opportunities to those who have resources to finance the election campaign.

TOO BIG TO FAIL

And now we come to the financial system and its dilemmas. First of all, it should be made clear that the Savings Banks were public financial entities. Much has been said about banks during the crisis, sometimes in very demagogic fashion. The first thing we should say, as Emilio Botín rightly said, is that the Savings Banks were public and that the private banks rode out the crisis much better than the Savings Banks. La Caixa, which was one of the Savings Banks which best managed the crisis, had a professional and competitive management which could be considered the equivalent of private management.

The wealth lost indirectly by Spanish people because of the collapse of their savings banks must be huge. Nobody has spoken about this topic, but the loss of wealth in this sense cannot have had an equivalent in any previous crisis.

Why did this happen? Why were the private companies better managed? The answer is very simple: because the money in public companies belongs to no one. Some directors of these companies supposedly used them for their personal gain because they were not controlled by shareholders. Fortunately, private companies did have this control by some of their shareholders and owners, and the management was more prudent and not in the interest of the company's managers.

This also happens with public bodies in general; the money belongs to no one and there are no incentives to save. This is why public-private management is a very good mechanism to allow governments to give their citizens the services they need. An example of this are approved schools. They generally provide better education and are cheaper than the public schools. The Obama Administration realised this, and promoted religious approved schools because they give better school performance and are cheaper for the State.

This can also be applied to the financial institutions. In fact, today, in some cases the Savings Banks have a mixed system similar to this one.

Returning to the theme of "Too big to fail". In the USA there has been a debate about the systemic risk posed by certain financial institutions, which can cause the country's whole financial system to fail. There has been talk of reducing the size of banks, and of dividing them. In 2010, the Obama administration approved the Dodd-Frank Wall Street Reform and Consumer Protection Act, designed to limit the size of banks which could become systemic.

In Spain there has been no serious debate about this topic and, moreover, it does not appear to be on the agenda to lighten the load of the next crisis. The fact is that, with the disappearance of many financial institutions, what has occurred is the opposite effect: there has been consolidation in the financial sector which is very negative for the country's economy. It is negative because it eliminates competitors and, consequently, takes power away from the consumer. But it is also particularly negative because it creates banks of a size much greater than the Spanish economy, with a great systemic risk.

Here we should not forget Ireland and what happened with its banks, or Iceland. When it comes down to it, we should consider whether it would not be a good idea to reduce the size of our financial institutions and oblige them by law to divide into smaller sizes.

Such a regulation should, perhaps, be on a European level, because it would make no sense to reduce the size of Spanish banks so that other larger ones were more competitive than ours. But I do believe that this is a debate we should have, and reducing the size of banks is an interesting proposition.

The idea of being too big to fail creates the perverse situation in which a large sized entity assumes more risks than it should because it knows it cannot fail; this poses a moral hazard.

PROTECTED HOUSING AND POORLY UNDERSTOOD PUBLIC INTERVENTION

It was Alberto Ruiz Gallardón's Popular Party which approved, in 2001, the Madrid Region land law. Much has been said about the Aznar Law which, frankly, had little effect on land because most of the regulation on this matter is a competence of the Autonomous Regions. Little has been said about the Land Laws in the Autonomous Regions, like the Gallardón law.

This law approved that more or less 45% of housing approved in a new sector, a new PAU (*Urban Development Plan*) as it was referred to, would be protected; in other words, with requirements or limits on access and with limits in terms of price. It considered that almost half the population of Madrid was entitled to a protected dwelling, which logically was paid for by the other inhabitants of Madrid who did not have one. It is obvious that there was no such need for protected housing. The limit on the sale price of flats also applied to land. The administration sold land below its market value so that flats could be sold below the market value. This meant also that the value of private land being developed went down because 45% was limited in terms of price.

The loss of resources for the Public Administration and everyone else caused by this measure has been enormous. This is not only because of the sale of Administration land below the market price (which has almost certainly also encouraged corruption, because these flats can be sold risk-free if they are in central areas of Madrid, at a price well below the market price, meaning that the person who buys it or is awarded the land is almost certainly doing good business), but also because income from VAT, stamp duty, municipal capital gains, etc. drops considerably when the sale price is limited.

What people found was that the criterion for buying a house in certain districts of Madrid depended more on cronyism, string-pulling or knowing one or other company or cooperative director, than the price. And when the price ceases to be the mechanism for allocating resources in markets, it is usually replaced by corruption. It creates perverse incentives for allocating the production factors and in the end means that the economy ends up badly.

But the real damage is in the loss of resources and, consequently, wealth from incoming taxes which have been lost with the sale of these protected houses to normal customers who could have bought another type of house.

I am not saying that protected housing is not necessary; I am simply saying that it is not necessary for 45% of the population. In my opinion, given that they are going to generate a loss in terms of opportunity cost for the Public Administration, it should be the

Public Administrations themselves which build the protected housing. Let's say that, for example, 10% of houses should be protected and they should be built by the Administration directly, with no private sector involvement, through non-profit making public companies created for the purpose. The remaining 90% should be offered at free market price. This would be much fairer and would generate resources, so that it would not be necessary to reduce social spending or take away civil servants' extra pay packets.

Whether this 10% should be owned or rented is another matter. Almost certainly the fairest way would be a rental system. A rent with a very low level of income, so that the 10% with the lowest income could improve their situation in the future. We could even create a fund for special situations which would defray the rent in certain cases so that their tenants did not have to pay it. This could apply in cases of unemployment, serious illness, etc.

Or perhaps the best solution is a free market in which those with lower earnings receive help to buy a house.

SUITABLE LEADERSHIP

I would like to take the opportunity here to talk about the importance of suitable leadership. In my professional experience, I have seen how leadership is acclaimed as a virtue which always leads to a good conclusion. But history is full of leaderships which have led to failure: Hitler, Mao and Stalin are just three examples among many of how leadership can lead a nation to ruin.

Following the right leader is fundamental; it is not sufficient to have a leader who concentrates all the popular ill-feeling to save us. Quite the contrary. Crisis situations require reflection and patience. We should be wary of charlatans with a friendly face. We have to take time to think and choose the leader we want for our country and the path we want to take.

I often see how the wrong leaders are acclaimed, for example in the case of Gowex. A leader has to be thoughtful, patient, and prudent, and must have knowledge and experience. This is not often found. Sometimes, if you want to set off to discover America, it is better to know nothing because if you know something you might never start off; but we should be aware that one thing is a high-risk business and another thing is a country, the future of its citizens, their children and their grandchildren.

A SPAIN WITH FUNDAMENTAL STRONG POINTS

You often hear many people say that Spain was living above its possibilities during the real estate boom, and in part they may be right. The mass influx of capital from overseas inflated the price of real estate assets. But it is also true to say that the growth the country has seen since the 1970s and especially since the 1980s is down to very solid fundamentals.

When my generation, the 70s generation, joined the employment market, we could still see older workers with very little qualification in computers, a very low or almost non-existent level of English, and so on. Our generation, the generation which studied EGB, was the first great change in the Spanish economy. It was a more qualified labour force which would become increasingly more qualified as the years went by.

Education for everyone, new technologies which made the world more global, like satellite dishes on which we could watch MTV, or computers, from the first Spectrum to the Amstrad and finally PCs, email, Internet, etc. The globalisation of communications and before that the modernising impulse of democracy have contributed to the fact that Spanish citizens on average are much better prepared than they were in the past.

Although the productivity statistics do not reflect this great change, it has occurred and Spanish companies have more qualified workers than before. There is still much to be done but, little by little, the number of qualified workers has increased and this has been clear to see in the growth of the Spanish economy since democracy.

Programmes such as Erasmus, or Spanish university graduates leaving to work in London or other European cities in middle management positions which require greater qualification, have contributed to greater international experience and to a much more open way of seeing the world.

The arrival of private universities with the Felipe Gonzalez Government contributed to extending technical knowledge beyond the exclusive public universities where the number of places was very limited. Studying engineering, for example, was only possible for those with the best results; fortunately, the arrival of private universities has allowed more people to study this type of degree, which are fundamental for the development of technology and businesses with added value which guarantee a country's future.

ARE PENSIONS SUSTAINABLE?

The answer is, in the long term, yes. Despite what is often believed, the level of technological growth in a capitalist economy where free competition takes priority is so high that the future of pensions is not in danger.

There is a popular belief that the population is getting older and it won't be possible to pay pensions in the future, but this is not true. You only have to take a look at history to realise that the evolution of technological growth is so great that it generates sufficient wealth to pay pensions without a problem.

The world today is much richer than it was a century ago and, unless there is a war or a catastrophe, it will be much richer in the future. Technology advances so quickly that it will generate sufficient yields to pay pensions in an ageing country. What's more, elderly people will be much more productive than they are today and will not need to live off their pension alone, but will be able to generate returns which create value for society as a whole. And if this were not enough, immigration will compensate for the ageing population.

DOES TECHNOLOGY GENERATE UNEMPLOYMENT?

The answer, clearly, is no. You only have to look at the countries which have lower unemployment (Japan, Germany, USA) compared to those which have most unemployment (Spain or Greece), to realise that technology does not generate unemployment. In fact, quite the contrary. This idea has already been explained by Yale Brozen, professor of Business Economics at the University of Chicago between 1957 and 1987. When an economy has a high technological component, the return from each worker increases substantially, which means that the company earns more money and, as a result, grows, reinvests in new business and in turn generates employment. A company which loses money is the company which does not hire personnel, whereas a company which earns a lot of money is the company which generates a lot of employment.

The same thing happens with a country: when it is a country with a high level of training, with businesses with high added value which export and receive great returns on their investments, in turn they reinvest in new business and generate more employment. When the businesses are not profitable, very cyclical or with very little added value, or have to pay a lot of taxes, little employment is created, the employment which is created is of low quality and in changes of cycle considerable unemployment is generated. This is what has happened in Spain during the crisis.

This is why it is very important to change the old mentality that technology generates unemployment. The mechanisation of factories generates profits and generates more, better quality employment in the future, even though an operator in that factory might lose his job to begin with.

As Luis Garicano explains very well in his book we have mentioned earlier, and as the Nobel prize-winner in economics Gary Becker has already studied, human capital is fundamental. The economy of knowledge is the future of a country. The productivity of the production factors which generate a nation's production depends on the efficiency of its workforce, and of the know-how of its managers. Good managers make a good company and good companies make a great country.

Cobb and Douglas, an economist and a mathematician from the University of Chicago who I spoke about earlier, carried out a study on a country's production and the factors on which it depends. In their regression analysis they showed that production depended on the Capital (not in terms of money but rather machinery, factories and so on) and on the workforce.

In this regression analysis, they highlighted a coefficient "A" which they called "total productivity of the production factors". When there was a change, or a "shock" as economists call it, in A, which increased its value, there was an increase in production and a simultaneous increase in workers' real salaries.

This is exactly what technology or a qualified workforce of managers does: they increase the production and increase workers' real salaries. In other words, the more technology there is and the more qualified the personnel is, the more we produce and the more we earn. This was not invented by Cobb and Douglas but was seen by analysing objective data and placing them in a statistical model to see their linear correlation. A linear regression.

It can be seen in Japan and Germany: more technology equals better salaries, more production and lower unemployment.

SHARING OUT THE CAKE: BUSINESSMAN AND WORKERS

Cobb and Douglas also saw that the percentage of production, or seen a different way, the income of a country, retained by the workers and retained by the capital, is usually the same when you look at different countries. It makes little difference whether we are talking about a communist country or a capitalist country. The portion taken by the capital and the portion taken by the workers is always a similar percentage.

So, what is the difference between a communist country and a capitalist country? The fundamental difference is in the size of the cake. And this is logical because any investor demands profitability. A communist country in which the State reallocates the resources as it sees fit or limits prices, in the long term usually has lower production growth than when the resources are allocated freely by individuals.

Let's not forget the Spanish case of the public Savings Banks and the private Banks. It is clear that the criteria for allocating resources are different in the two cases.

You only have to look at China to realise that when an economy allows its resources to be reallocated more freely, it grows more and generates more wealth. The healthy growth in this country's economy is down to so many years of communism, which distributed the production resources inefficiently. Once China changed and began to liberalise its economy, production started to increase and the country started to grow until it became what it is today.

Economic freedom is fundamental if a country is to grow. Anything which limits it means more poverty for its citizens. You only have to look at North Korea, Venezuela or Cuba to see that the State does not allocate the production factors correctly and does not generate the wealth generated by a liberalised capitalist economy.

Here we should not confuse public spending as a percentage of GDP with a liberalised economy or an interventionist economy. Venezuela may have lower public spending as a percentage of GDP than Spain's and, yet, have an interventionist economy or a planned economy compared to Spain.

In other words, when we say that Denmark has public spending which is 57% of its GDP, we are not talking about a planned economy; Venezuela, however, which has public spending which is approximately 30% of its GDP, is a planned economy. The production factors are allocated through state planning and not freely in the market. A State can spend a lot of money yet, when it comes to spending it, do so in a free market. As an example, we could ensure that any public tender is carried out in free competition conditions and with appropriate honourability. A State can spend money on health and, for example, subcontract its management between the different operators competing to provide that service.

As Pedro Schwartz explains very well in his book "The economy explained to Zapatero and his successors in two afternoons"[15], liberalisation is not the same as privatisation. In fact, very often States privatise to obtain financing but do not liberalise, with the consequent harm for consumers. All they do is fill the coffers with the sale of public assets.

Liberalisation allows there to be free competition and for operators to bid different prices. This means that the service should be allocated according to the quality-price ratio.

If the 20th century was the century in which workers' socialism triumphed, the 21st century will be the century in which

---

[15] Pedro Schwartz. "La economía explicada a Zapatero y a sus sucesores en dos tardes". Ed. S.L.U. Espasa Libros, 2011

consumer socialism triumphs. Countries like the USA, where free competition allows consumers to enjoy products and services at a low price, are the benchmark for the rest of the world. It is now no longer important just to have good salaries, but also to have low prices.

THE PROBLEM OF THE HIGH COST OF ENERGY

The high cost of energy effects the productivity of work and, consequently, brings about less production and lower salaries for the workforce producing it. An economy like the Spanish economy, which has a high energy dependence and which also has a high cost of energy, produces less and has workers with lower salaries.

It is important for us to know this: in other words, if we produced cheaper energy, such as nuclear energy for example, the salaries of Spanish workers would be higher. By turning our backs on nuclear energy we are turning our backs on earning more and producing more.

This is not a value judgement on my behalf, but simply a description of what is happening. When renewable energies are subsidised it increases the total cost of the energy and,

138

consequently, the total production of the economy and workers' salaries go down.

Having said this, it is now time for the country to decide whether it prefers to have lower salaries and reduce the risk of a nuclear disaster, or whether it prefers to have lower salaries to have less contaminating energies which do not contribute to climate change.

A combination of the two has to be something strategic which the country should decide with as broad a consensus as possible, so that there are no sudden shifts. A decision like this must take into account the risks, the sustainability of the energy, its cost and its impact on total production, on what the workers are going to earn or, possibly, the number of workers there will be. In other words, the cheaper and better the energy, the more money is earned and more employment created and, consequently, there is less unemployment.

With technology, sometimes being a pioneer is not an advantage, and this is what has happened with the installation of solar panels in Spain. We have subsidised them to increase the percentage of our mix of renewable energies and in doing so we have increased the cost of our energy; we have installed less efficient panels than those which have been produced subsequently and we have ended up exporting the engineers who learned from this boom in renewable energies to other countries, where they are sharing our knowledge. In this sense we have been pioneers and we have exported our knowledge, but almost certainly the total cost for an economy like the Spanish one, with high unemployment and low salaries, has been excessive. We would all like to have a detached house in our city's best neighbourhood, but the question is whether we can afford it or not. The stake placed by Zapatero's government on renewable energies, while positive, should have been less ambitious. The final cost is lower salaries in the long term and when these cannot be reduced, more unemployment.

The next government inherited a problem with a high cost for the country. The solution it provided does not appear to be the right solution for a serious government either.

The ideal solution would have been a more moderate and strategic stake on renewable energies. It should have been agreed between the two major political parties. Bearing in mind the problem of international terrorism, nuclear energy does not appear to be the best solution. We will have to see how we can reduce the cost of energy. Perhaps this stake on renewable energies will in the future develop an industry which will allow us to reduce Spain's overseas energy dependence. It is obvious that Spain should earmark a considerable budget for R+D+I related to renewable energies, particularly solar energy, given that it is a country with a large number of cloudless days a year.

MINIMUM WAGE AND ITS IMPACT ON EMPLOYMENT

Economists are well aware that establishing a minimum wage influences the level of unemployment. When an economy like Spain's, which has low productivity because it is very much associated with low added value services, such as cheap sun and sand tourism, too high a minimum wage generates unemployment.

The same happens in economic crises: the real estate sector is very cyclical because buying a house is an investment which requires job safety so that people can meet their mortgage payments. When confidence falls, investors stop buying houses. This means that construction workers cannot produce more because there is usually an excess of stock at the end of the cycle. These workers then join the dole queue, and here we have a new problem: their low qualifications mean they are unable to find a job, and the fact that there is a minimum wage for hiring a worker means that finding work is even more difficult. This is the case because they do not produce enough to be profitable for the companies which want to hire them. What happens is that when these workers are no longer claiming unemployment benefit, they start to work on the black market, or relocate to other sectors, for example working in a bar, sometimes being paid under the counter because it is not profitable to hire them and pay them a minimum wage plus taxes.

This means that economies like the Spanish economy have a high level of tax fraud. This is because its economy has grown with domestic demand in sectors which produce little, such as the example of our bar.

Compared to this, an economy like Germany, which is more industrial and exports more than 40% of its GDP, is an economy which is much easier to control in terms of taxes. Exports are controlled more easily, because they have to go through customs and more controls. Normally, exporting companies are competitive overseas and that is why they export, and this is due to the fact that they generate a greater added value. They tend to hire more qualified workers and the minimum wage regulation affects them less.

In other words, in addition to the fact that we might think that Greeks or Spanish have a greater tendency for tax fraud, the reality is that if they exported more they would have to declare what they export and there would be much less fraud, which is what is happening now. What's more, as they would earn more money they would pay higher salaries and there would be fewer workers being paid under the counter.

Almost certainly the Protestant work ethic also has something to do with the fact that the Germans commit less fraud, but I don't think this is the only reason. I think that this ethic has more of an influence on their frugality and on their consumption patterns, which means that they tend to be bigger savers and not to consume more than they produce.

Whatever the case, in my opinion, it is necessary to have a certain minimum wage because it serves as a floor for company hiring. This means that those who are just below this figure tend to earn more when they earn the minimum wage. Logically, those who are considerably below it will earn money illegally or won't work at all. This is why is important to establish a minimum wage which is not too high.

THE IMPORTANCE OF GENERATING CONFIDENCE WITH INTERNATIONAL INVESTORS

Becoming part of the single European currency meant that the countries which were in it could not devalue their currency to improve their trade terms and thereby solve their foreign deficit problems. This means that the smaller and more peripheral countries, like Greece, Cyprus, Portugal, Ireland, Spain and so on, some of which have a very negative trade balance, such as Greece, had no other mechanism than to devalue real salaries to be able to export and thereby correct the imbalances.

When countries like Spain had very restrictive employment legislation, this devaluation took the form of firing workers. Companies reduced their costs by making people redundant. Salaries went down because there were fewer people working. During the crisis, when the employment legislation was more inflexible, salaries went up with the CPI, which increased employment costs, thereby worsening company losses and causing more unemployment. When Mariano Rajoy's government made the employment market more flexible, real salaries started to fall and gradually this imbalance was corrected. The result of this is that the economy is expected to grow by 3% in 2015. This is not just because of a decrease in salaries, but also because by lowering the price of land and properties, foreign investors invest in the country and also provide it with financing. The crisis finds a floor thanks to overseas sales and the fact that foreigners buy or invest in the country. For this to happen there needs to be a correction in the prices of the country's production factors but there also needs to be confidence. This has not happened in Greece.

THE PUBLIC-PRIVATE ECONOMIC SYSTEM

The US economy is one of the most competitive and efficient, a highly liberalised economy which allocates resources by quality and price. It is a very privatised economy. But when you travel there, you are surprised to find people living on the street with nowhere else to sleep, or very dangerous areas with high criminality which are only kept stable through police control. This does not happen in Europe. Or if it does, it is to a lesser degree.

It is clear that Social Democrat and Christian Democrat policies in Europe have generated rights and services for its citizens. This is a welfare state which has to be maintained and which, for certain countries, may be unsustainable in the short and medium term. In my opinion the European model is the winner, and Latin America would be a much better place if they had managed to implement the European model and not use the US model as a reference. On this point I agree with José Carlos Díez, as I have already said.

In Spain we have quality public and private health. The private system is not as efficient and as good as the one in the USA, precisely because the production factors are not allocated by price. In other words, you do not pay 100% of what private health really "costs" because it has to compete with the public health system, and if it were excessively expensive there would be no benefit in going private, or it would be better to go to the USA. This mixed system, both in Health and in Education, ensures that private education is cheaper and public education is of good quality. Doctors in the public system, furthermore, have the incentive to do things well so that they can set up their own private consultancy.

It is a system which means that doctors do not earn what they deserve and the patients do not pay directly everything they should pay (they pay via taxes), but in my opinion it is quite a good system. In fact, I think it is the best system for citizens as a whole. Perhaps the US system is better for those who can pay for it, but the Spanish system is reasonably good, both for those who can pay and for those who cannot.

CAN SPAIN BE DENMARK?

Honestly, I don't think so. Denmark is very close to the Ruhr basin, the most populated and richest area in Europe. It is easy to set up a country which exports to that region and which lives off its trade surpluses. It then takes the surpluses and invests them in an excellent education system and in creating an industry of high added value. This is easy given its location. In fact, this is what happens in Catalonia, although on a smaller scale. Many people say that the Catalans are hard workers and good business people, but how many people are there in Catalonia from other regions who could also fit this description?

Spain is not where Denmark is. If you look at Andalusia, it is difficult to imagine how, given its location, it could export a great deal. The day that Africa develops, perhaps Andalusia will be an exporting power, although maybe the opposite will happen, and North Africa will export to an Andalusia which has developed through tourism and by exporting to the richer regions of Spain which have grown.

Spain won't be Denmark. But we can copy some things from them, such as stimulating the industry with added value in the regions closest to northern Europe. This is a phenomenon which is already occurring by its very nature and, in fact, the Catalans and the Basques have high-level universities (Esade, Pompeu Fabra, Deusto and so on). Wealth generates wealth and investment in education, which generates further wealth.

Catalonia and the Basque country have grown considerably because of their geographical location. This is because they are closer to the south of France, with costs which are, let's say, 20-25% cheaper than there; they also have a cheaper workforce originating in the more depressed regions of Spain (Andalusia,

Extremadura, etc.). This is the origin of the development of industry in Catalonia and the Basque country.

This is why it makes no sense now for them to become independent. They have taken advantage of a cheap labour force from the rest of Spain and the fact that they are in Spain, and now they cannot say: "now that we can't take any more cheap labour from the rest of Spain, but instead from Morocco or Latin American countries, we no longer want to show solidarity with the poorer regions". And we are going to vote on it. It would be like asking rich people to vote on whether taxes should be reduced in the middle of a crisis. They would certainly vote yes, as they no longer need poor people to get along.

It would be unfair, now that the workforce does not come from the rest of Spain, and they are developing industries with a greater added value, to demand independence because the other regions are living off them. It is not fair and it is a decision which should be taken by everyone affected. In other words, by the whole of Spain, as the Constitution clearly states.

This is not to take anything away from Catalan or Basque businesses. It is obvious that they have worked well and have educated their children with the benefits of their industries. Here it is difficult to say whether the chicken or the egg came first.

Whether the Catalans have been great entrepreneurs because they were close to Europe and have attracted entrepreneurial talent, or because of their very nature and their culture. I tend to believe that is a mixture of the two, but their location takes precedence. There are almost certainly great Andalusian entrepreneurs in Catalonia who went there because of the opportunities generated by an economy which exported to Europe.

FISCAL POLICIES: RISES AND FALLS IN PUBLIC SPENDING, RISES AND FALLS IN TAXATION

The analysis of the different economic policy measures a country can take is complex and I am not going to go into too much detail. I will simply talk about the short-term impact of the measures, which is what really matters right now in the middle of a crisis.

The tax rises requested by Brussels had a negative impact in the short term on the domestic demand of the Spanish economy and, consequently, made the fall in GDP even worse. This, in turn, brought about an increase in public deficit as a percentage of GDP. In fact, the crisis really took a turn for the worse in Europe in 2010, when they started taking these pro-cyclical measures which stimulated the fall of the economy even further.

Exactly the same thing happened with the decrease in public spending: there is a contraction in the domestic demand of the country's economy, it sells less, it produces less and more unemployment is generated.

The consequence of these measures can be seen clearly in 2013, when unemployment in Europe was at its highest level.

Decreased taxes or increased public spending have the opposite effect, although in a crisis of confidence like the one we have at the moment, it appears more reasonable to increase public spending because the money goes directly to increasing domestic demand; if you reduce taxes, however, a part of it goes to paying off debt and part to the savings of families who do not consume because of fear and consequently do not generate domestic demand which causes companies and employment to grow. In other words, the best measure to take in a crisis of this type from the point of view of fiscal policy is to increase public spending. Just the opposite of what Brussels is asking for. And as we emerge from the crisis, which seems to be what is happening now, perhaps it would be best to reduce taxes.

In the long term, the situation is different: low levels of public spending and taxes maximise the potential growth of an economy because private individuals allocate the resources better.

An economy with free markets and low taxes is an economy which grows more than others with more regulated markets and high taxes. But this does not mean that markets must not be regulated and that taxes must always be low. When a market is not regulated, as happened in the financial market in the crisis of 2009, it is easy for disproportionate risks to be taken or for levels of fairness to be very low.

Let's take as an example the professional football market. The best players earn astronomical amounts if you compare them with the players in the second division. They earn so much that sometimes it is questionable whether it might not be better to have players with a more or less similar level, but earning less. They are totally free markets. The same happens with the managers of large private companies. In the end, it is more than questionable whether the astronomical amounts that can be earned, for example, by fund managers make any sense. Here, in my opinion, we have to introduce a certain level of regulation which places limits on salaries and brings the salaries of the worst paid closer to the better paid. It seems that a certain level of fairness is necessary.

The same thing happens in society as a whole: markets must have restrictions which guarantee social justice, and at the same time they will be beneficial for growth. The fact that the 20th century was the century of greatest economic growth after the birth of socialism in the 19th century is no accident. The existence of equal opportunities and social balance is necessary for an economy to grow in a healthy manner (you only have to see the opposite case in Latin America, to realise that a lack of fairness ends up with low levels of growth or communist regimes which discourage production).

Consequently, it is evident that markets and economies must have a certain level of regulation and public intervention, when necessary, to soften the effects of economic cycles. If, instead of the de Guindos Decrees, countercyclical measures had been taken during the crisis, it would not have been so serious in 2013 and we would not have had such poor growth in 2014 and 2015.

The same thing happens with public spending. Let's take Latin America as an example. If, during the most recent decade of growth in Latin American economies, the States had invested in infrastructures, education and health, that investment would have increased the growth potential of their economies. When an economy does not have productive investment in its future, either because of low levels of training or other reasons, public intervention is required to make those investments. In fact, the history of Spain is awash with major public investments which have improved the country's competitiveness. Examples of these are the public investment in Christopher Columbus's voyage, the Academies of Philip V, the investment made by "Madrid's finest mayor" Charles III, the creation of the National Institute of Industry in Franco's time, Felipe Gonzalez's investment in motorways and the high-speed train (AVE), José Maria Aznar's modernisation of Madrid airport, etc. Public investment is fundamental.

Today more than ever, as I have already said, it is important for public investment in Spain to focus on university education and professional training, and on research.

Epilogue: the future of Spain

Promoting an exporting economy is essential. Consequently, Catalonia and the Basque country are regions which will be at an advantage. This will be the only way we will be able to pay our debts. It will generate political and social imbalances, and all the political parties must contribute to correcting these. Solidarity between territories and between sectors of the population is a necessity in Spain. Without this the country will not be sustainable.

An exporting industrial economy, even if it is richer, generates more social differences than an economy based on the services sector and on domestic demand.

The risk of the arrival of communism as a result of high levels of unemployment, and the risk of a desire for independence arising from the fact that there is less money to share out between the Autonomous Regions are the two major problems facing Spain in the future.

It appears that Spain's future route will involve that struggle between more or less solidarity between territories or more or less solidarity between generations and between social groups with different levels of income. This solidarity will be the key; if we manage to achieve the correct balance which means that in the end we all work better, and are more productive, it will mean that we are all richer and happier. Peace between territories and between social classes is necessary if the country is to prosper.

There also needs to be freedom and equal opportunities, and for people who work well to receive their just reward. People who want to gain qualifications should be able to do so, whether or not they have the economic resources. This is essential if we want the best engineers to come from the highest or the lowest social class, and not be the son or daughter of the Dean of the Faculty or of the person with the means to pay for it.

Equal opportunities are precisely what have most deteriorated in Spain in the last twenty years, and this is something we have to return to. To that dream which began with democracy and with the election victory of Felipe Gonzalez. Equal opportunities for everyone and work. Public investment in education, research and development, not just in quantity but also in efficiency and competitiveness.

We need stimuli and facilities to ensure that private investment goes in the same direction. In the long term private investment is more efficient and, I would say, more intelligent. The richest societies tend to invest in training and in research. People are not stupid and know that training is fundamental. People see that their engineer neighbour lives better than the man digging on the worksite. People know that we need investment in training. In fact, anyone who can normally invests a greater part of their disposable income on education for their children than a country does on its GDP, and if they do not do so it is because they can send their child to a quality public or approved school.

In this economy, which some of us call the knowledge economy, as Luis Garicano points out very well in "Spain's dilemma", the best trained and the best overall will have the best jobs (just look at Cristiano Ronaldo and Messi today). There will also be work for those working in sectors which require direct contact with the customer or where it is profitable to have a person because of the manual complexity of the work. But the latter will be the first to go to the dole queue in times of crisis. Training is the key in Spain and we have to bring ourselves up to date.

THE SERVICE VOCATION AND RESPECT FOR IDEAS

I wanted to finish this discussion by talking about the vocation of serving others and the respect for ideas. The vocation of customer service is something which is increasing in capitalist economies. The more competition there is, the more important it is to treat the customer well. This is what I call customer socialism. You can see this very clearly when you study in an American university. The teachers and professors are much more attentive and much more accessible than teachers and professors in Spanish universities. I believe this culture of customer service arises from the competitive nature of the US economy itself. If a professor wants to be successful, he or she has to provide a good service to the students, who are the people who will evaluate him/her and will pay a considerable sum of money to study at that university.

In Spain professors tend to be more distant (of course, I am talking in general), almost certainly because, once they have become a professor, the way they are assessed by the students is not important. A professor who fails half of his or her class would have very little future at Harvard, Chicago or Stanford. In Spain that person is a professor with prestige within the faculty. There is obviously a lack of competition in this system.

Respect for ideas is also a problem in our country. In the Anglo-Saxon world, in general terms the impression is that there is greater respect for other people's ideas. Even when they are not shared, people tend to be more respectful of other people's ideology. Here, insults on the radio or in the press are commonplace when someone from a different ideology is in government.

We have to learn to listen and respect what other people say even if we don't agree with them. The Spanish have to realise that the more moderate nations, those which take decisions with a cool head, are those with the best future. Being angry all the time with someone who has a different opinion from you leads you nowhere.

This would appear to be a matter of minor importance, but I disagree: the future depends on ideas, and if ideas are to triumph they have to be listened to, shared, processed and built on.

158

www.ingramcontent.com/pod-product-compliance
Lightning Source LLC
Chambersburg PA
CBHW032025170526
45157CB00002B/855